40 DAY DEVOTIONAL WITH DECREES

UNBREAKABLE EMBRACE

DESTROY THE SEPARATION MINDSET & DIVE INTO THE ARMS OF A HAPPY DADDY GOD

CHRISTA ELISHA JOY SCHRAM

Copyright © 2022 by Christa Elijah Joy Schram ISBN: 9798408135547
Imprint: Independently published

Cover Design by Christa Elisha Joy Schram All rights reserved. No part of this book may be reproduced without permission from the publisher, except by a reviewer who may quote brief passages in a review. Nor may any part of this book be reproduced, stored in a retrieval system, or copied by mechanical, photocopying, recording or other means, without permission in writing from the publisher.

Cry Out Ministries International P.O. Box 103 Webster, IN 47392 Printed in the United States of America Scripture quotations marked TPT are from The Passion Translation®. Copyright © 2017, 2018, 2020 by Passion & Fire Ministries, Inc. Used by permission. All rights reserved. ThePassionTranslation.com.

Scripture quotations taken from the Amplified® Bible (AMP), Copyright © 2015 by The Lockman Foundation. Used by permission. www.lockman.org"

Scripture quotations marked (NLT) are taken from the Holy Bible, New Living Translation, copyright ©1996, 2004, 2015 by Tyndale House Foundation. Used by permission of Tyndale House Publishers, Carol Stream, Illinois 60188. All rights reserved. x

DEDICATION

I dedicate this book to my wonderful Father God who sent his only Son, Jesus, and his precious Holy Spirit, on the most epic rescue mission in all time and eternity, to bring me back home to him. His love has changed my life and continues to wreck all my religiosity. I also want to dedicate this book to my parents. Daddy, your dad's Name??, thanks for teaching me to work hard, laugh a lot, dance for fun, honor God and fight for those I love. To my mom in heaven, thank you for teaching me that "Jesus loves me" is the axis on which my world turns, that worship is a weapon, and that a mustard seed of faith moves mountains. She cultivated my gifts, both natural and supernatural, and I know that she is still cheering me on from the grandstands of heaven. To my husband, David who is my rock and my spell checker. And, to the many spiritual mothers and fathers who have poured into our lives, particularly Poppa Scott and Momma Ann Smith, who have adopted us as their own and who are responsible for starting my first YouTube channel. Finally, our Apostle, Poppa Urie Hershberger, who has taught us that being the least in the kingdom is the greatest calling of all. Thank you.

ENDORSEMENTS

From the moment that I met her, I knew that Christa was an emerging prophetic voice. She had done the hard stuff and had come out the other side. God was not only raising her up as a voice to America but to the nations! Since that time, I have had the pleasure of calling Christa my friend. I've said it many times to many people: Christa is the real deal! Transparent. Humble. Kind. Brave. Bold. She is also a gifted teacher! There is no one that I personally know who grasps the Father's heart like Christa does. As detailed in her book, she knows the sorrow of walking away from the Lord, and the immeasurable joy of His loving arms welcoming her back. She has tasted and seen His goodness and truly walks with Him. Throughout my life, I have read many devotionals. Believe me when I say that this is unlike any devotional I have ever read. It's practical, layered, and fun! Without fail, each day was exactly what I needed. I couldn't keep my eyes from welling up with tears as I received the Father's heart for me. This book is truly anointed to take you deeper into the Father's love! Set some time away every day to fully immerse yourself in Unbreakable Embrace; read it aloud as she suggests, and you will leave changed for the better!

Jeff Tharp
Host of ElijahFire

Christa's book, Unbreakable Embrace, is a journey into the heart of God. As I read this devotional, I was reminded of the time I was leading worship and I was crying out, "Open up your heart and let me in!" Suddenly, in the Spirit, it was no longer Jesus asking me to open up my heart and let Him in. It was me asking Jesus to open up His hear and let me in! In that moment, I opened the door of Jesus' heart and became fully surrounded by His heart. When I read this devotional, I hear the heartbeat of God resonating– I sense His presence and I am made aware of His power. In this 40-day devotional, you will read God's thoughts over you each day and then you will activate what you have read by decrees that Christa has written. These decrees are key to breaking off any inferiority complex that is over your life and reminds you that you are highly valued in the kingdom of God. Each day also gives you an opportunity to write out what the LORD is speaking over you for that day. "Unbreakable Embrace" is a fresh word from heaven that will lead you out of the wilderness and into the land of His promises.

Christopher Monaghan
Translator of the Name Translation Bible (TNT)
Pastor of Gateway Church, Richmond, Indiana

I felt blessed that Christa was obedient to the Lord in documenting and sharing her sacred moments and her experiences with Daddy God. By Christa sharing her devotions, I was lifted to a new awareness that I too could experience the Father's love on a much higher level than ever before. Christa awakened in me the reality that God truly is my Father and that I should never hide my sin, my thinking or my emotions from Daddy God. Unbreakable Embrace encourages me to lay it all down at His feet and allow Him to comfort, encourage, and speak to me.

Sue Knox Eason
Author of "Spirit Enemies"

FORWARD

This book has taken me over a year to write. You would think that a 40-day devotional shouldn't take much longer than the 40 days that it covers, right? Well, let me get honest with you here; the reason this book took so long for me to complete is because when I initially started writing it, I didn't know I was writing a book. What you will read in each daily devotional began as a compilation of my own secret place encounters with God during seasons of intense loss, grief, betrayal, and spiritual warfare.

In this season of emotional crushing, my heart was broken and the lies from the enemy threatened to overwhelm me. It was all I could do most days to just sit in my recliner, call on the Lord and ask him to come hold me and heal me. I could so deeply relate to King David as I read the psalms and saw him crying out to God for a Father's help. It was in the running for his life in the wilderness and hiding in caves that David learned to lean into the Father's embrace. He would pour out his heart and the Lord would listen and respond to David in a way that melted away all the arrows of accusation, dismantled all his fears, replaced insecurity with boldness, reminded him of his identity, infused his soul with hope, imparted wisdom to rule and conquer as a king and ultimately delivered him from all his enemies. The same was and is true for me.

I began to document some of my exchanges with the Lord, for my own personal reference. Then one day he told me to share some of my encounters on my Facebook page as corporate prophetic words of comfort over his people. The response to these posts was overwhelming evidence that God was indeed ministering to his people through reading the word in the same way he had ministered to me as I was receiving it. He then instructed me that it was his desire to have me compile all my encounters with him in order to create a devotional that would lead others into the same kind of intimacy that he and I shared. God has the best ideas. It wasn't until I had the full 40 days of devotionals finished that I asked God what the theme of this book was about. It sounds so silly, doesn't it? That a person would write a book without even knowing what the theme was? But I truly didn't! This was God's idea, not mine. I was only being obedient. But as I began to read through each day, I could feel the lump in my throat and tears of joy well up in my eyes. I could see now what he had been doing all along.

Each day he was specifically addressing a father wound that spoke directly to my identity. And why father wounds? Because fathers impart identity to their children. If we don't know who we are to our father, we become susceptible to the lies of the accuser. The moment we believe a lie is when we are susceptible to fall into sin, since pain always seeks pleasure. God knows better than anyone, that the number one tactic of the enemy to get a believer to fall from grace is to get them to doubt who they are as his dearly loved children. (See Genesis 3)

The book of Revelation says that "We overcome Satan (the accuser) by the blood of the lamb and the word of our testimony." Again, in Revelation it says, "The spirit of prophecy is the testimony of Jesus" The word testimony in Greek means to "be an eye witness" and in the Hebrew means "to do it again with the same power and authority." This is so powerful guys!

This means when we see what Jesus has done for someone else, he is willing to do it again for us with the same power and authority! This is why the Lord commanded the Israelites to not only keep the commandments, but also the
testimony, (Duet. 6:17) so that they could bear witness for other generations to experience similar victories and breakthroughs.

This book is my testimony. It is a vulnerable look into my secret place process. What you are about to embark on is a 40-day eyewitness account of seeing the Father's face as I pour my heart out to him. As you read, you will see him the same way as I do. He will come wipe away your tears, remind you who you are, assure you of his presence and acceptance in the midst of pain, persecution and rejection. He will give you wisdom and comfort, heal you from trauma, and bind up your broken heart. He will give you beauty for ashes, joy for mourning and praise for heaviness. He will deliver you from all your enemies and lead you into triumphant victory ready to share your own testimony. Are you ready? I hope so! There is a lost and hurting world that is hungry and waiting for someone to introduce them to a good God and loving Father.

INTRODUCTION

As a child I knew Jesus. In fact, some of the earliest memories I have are of communicating with him as a friend and taking trips to heaven to play during my nap times. Interacting with Jesus and the spiritual realm has always been my normal. I assume this was the sovereign will of God to gift me in this way, but I have always wondered if it is in some part due to the unusual circumstances surrounding my conception.

It was the beginning of the new year 1984, that my parents, who had been separated and prepared to file for divorce, had a radical encounter with God that saved their marriage. They were young high school sweethearts who became teenage parents and married right after graduation. There was trauma and bitterness on both sides of the family surrounding my mom's pregnancy with my oldest sister. Long story short, no one thought their marriage would last and some didn't want it to. Before age 21 my mom had three little children with my dad, one of which was disabled after a freak accident. With no college education or public assistance, they constantly struggled.

My dad was always more of a reactionary man rather than a planner. He has always barreled through life, recklessly taking on whatever odds were stacked against him. His motto is "If there is a will then there is a way." Although both my parents had strong Christian grandparents neither of them was born again. The failing marriage left my dad's will broke. The Spirit of God gripped my father's heart one cold December night when he was missing his wife and children at Christmas. He repented and asked God to save his marriage and give him his family back. He pursued my mother with the same unrestraint he had during their freshman year at Ross High School. Mom would later tell me that the first time she ever heard Jesus's love for her was through my father, who would show up every day to bring her gifts with tears in his eyes, proclaiming his vows of unconditional love for her only to be met with the slam of the door in his face. The love of God working through my dad eventually won over my mother. She invited my father home and they both invited Jesus into their hearts. That week my mother and father spontaneously were baptized in the Holy Spirit, and I was conceived as a sign of their new covenant of love with Christ at the center of their marriage. My parents, not realizing it prophetically, named me Christa Elisha Joy, which means "Christ is my salvation and joy."

I assume I received the Holy Spirit the same time my mother did, that resulted in such an uncommon relationship with Jesus, even as a baby, since the primary function of Holy Spirit is to reveal Jesus as the Son of God. Regardless of knowing Jesus as friend and Holy Spirit as his presence with me, the concept of Father God was very foreign to me. In fact, the Father scared me somewhat.

He scared me because the only gospel I was told was the message that humans were wretched sinners saved by grace. The Father that I imagined was far away from me and was portrayed as this angry God that required an innocent sacrifice to be appeased. He was a confusing character that I had a healthy reverence for and equally unhealthy ignorance of. Jesus seemed to be the only thing between me and this angry Father who hated my sin and required blood to atone for it.

The older I got the more aware of my sin I became. My pure little heart wanted so much to make my parents and God happy, yet I always found myself falling short. The birth of my little brothers only made matters worse in that they were always getting into something they were not supposed to be in. As the older of the three (in what I call my parent's second set of children, since there was such a large age gap from their previous separation) I was usually the one taking the fall, not only for my own hyperactive impulsivity, but also for theirs. To top it off, my poor old dad had hearing loss from being in a loud work environment all day, so when he spoke, he would often yell simply because he couldn't hear. I was a sensitive child, and this alone made it seem as if I were always in trouble, even if I was not. I know now that the enemy capitalized on every opportunity to use my natural father to reinforce lies that I would subconsciously transfer to my understanding of Father God. Untreated Post- traumatic stress disorder (PTSD) from sexual abuse by an older boy that resulted in a still born pregnancy at thirteen years old, sent me on a downward spiral of self-destruction. With the introduction of serious trauma in my life, these lies only continued to pile up. Much like the dirty laundry that littered my bedroom floor as a clinically depressed teenager, the door of my heart was blocked by fear, unforgiveness, shame and unimaginable pain, keeping the revelation of the Father's love far from me. My inner world with all its chaos felt like the proverbial "pigsty" my parents often told me I was living in.

Much of my teenage years I spent as a run-away. Not only from my parents who I resented, but also away from God. After all, how in the world could he possibly love me if he allowed me to go through so much pain? Little did I know that Jesus said in John 10:10, The thief comes to kill, steal, and destroy but I came so that you might have abundant life. The truth I discovered later was that Father God was not punishing me for being a bad girl when bad things happened. Bad things happened to me because I was God's chosen girl who the enemy had set out to destroy to keep me from discovering my identity. The veiled reality was that the Father sent his Son on the most epic rescue mission in all time and eternity so that I could become adopted into his royal family and become a beloved child of God, fully empowered to destroy hell. What a worm the devil is, to abuse the pure and innocent and then deceive them into believing it was God who was their abuser.

Even in my running away, The Father's love pursued me, as did the prayers of my parents who didn't know what to do to save me. The Father was there every time I hit rock bottom and cried out for his help. He supernaturally persevered my life through a near drowning, a kidnapping, multiple overdoses, several suicide attempts, gun misfires, horrific domestic abuse, a roll over collision, a botched spinal procedure and many more things that only my over worked guardian angels know of. Finally in February of 2012, after twenty years of running and shutting God out of my messy heart, I came to my senses and turned back to God in desperate need of a savior. He was faithful to come running to meet me on my prodigal road and I have never looked back at the pigsty I once lived in.

Those first years of my salvation, my relationship with Jesus and Holy Spirit, picked right up where it had left off. Unfortunately, my overwhelming sense of separation from the Father and the looming fear of his disappointment toward me picked back up as well. I was constantly focusing on my sin nature in a pitiful attempt to control it. This was futile because humans were designed by God to look like what they look at. (Genesis 2:7) If I had known this, I would have spent my time looking at the Father in unhindered worship rather than looking at my sin and trying to find ways I could work my way into the Father's pleasure. My effort to prove to the Father that I loved him and was worthy of his love ended in me being burnt out with religious activities and just as depressed as I was prior to my salvation.

Yet again, Daddy God stepped in with divine intervention to rescue me. It came by way of an opportunity to attend a conference in Orlando Florida. It was certainly a financial miracle for me at the time to be able to go. I had never been away from my husband or children and I was terrified of being alone. Yet the thought of continuing in the state I was in was even more dismal. I made up my mind that I would do whatever it took to experience the abundant life Jesus said that he came to give me.

So, to Florida I went to listen to a preacher named Bill Johnson, who I had never heard of before. The first night of the conference, the air seemed to crackle with supernatural expectancy. I had never experienced an atmosphere that was so thick with the Glory of God. During the most intimate corporate worship set I had ever encountered before, I heard my friend, Holy Spirit, whisper in my ear, "If you want to be set free you must release yourself. Forgive heart. I felt the crushing spirit of heaviness lift off my shoulders! My tears turned into ecstatic joy as I felt freedom flood my soul! I could hardly sit in my seat, but worship ended, and the first speaker of the evening was introduced.

I could see his white hair as the stage lights glistened off his glasses. Bill Johnson opened his session with his stoic demeanor, steady voice and standard three family friendly jokes, and then he began to lay out from Genesis to Revelation a gospel I had never heard before. It was the story of the Father on a rescue mission to bring his lost sons and daughters home.

As Bill spoke it felt as if a veil was lifted off my face and I could recognize the Father through the person of Jesus for the very first time. We went into a time of corporate prayer at the end of the sermon. An adorable couple prayed and began to prophesy over me. All I remember next was this beautiful, little, soft-spoken lady giving me a hug and saying, "The Father is going to hug you now and he is never going to let you go." What happened next can only be described as what Jesus must have experienced coming out of the Jordan River at his baptism! The heavens opened and the Father's love crashed over me in relentless waves of divine ecstasy! His love pressed down on me and simultaneously burst through me like bolts of lightning!

Then I heard him say "Christa, you aren't in trouble anymore darling. You are my daughter in who I find great joy! Christa, you make me HAPPY!" I could see him now, my beautiful Father, arms outstretched reaching out to me! I could see myself in the twinkle of his eyes and feel the warmth of his shining smile over me. I knew now that the Father was my friend just like Jesus was my friend, because Jesus and the Father are one! I knew that every time I heard the voice of Holy Spirit, I was hearing the voice of my Daddy God because the Holy Spirit will not speak on his own accord, but only what he hears from the Father. I could see that it was the Father who had chased me down and overwhelmed me with salvation kisses on my prodigal road, and it had been the Father who had led me to that very seat to open my ears and my eyes to the reality of his unconditional, unimaginable, incomprehensible love for me. For three days I was held in this unexplainable rapture that at some points became so overwhelming I thought that I might die if he released any more of his love over me. I suppose I did die through that encounter- my old life died, and I was truly born again. I knew what it meant to be a new creation in Christ (2 Corinthians 5:17) and had received the spirit of adoption so that I could call God, Abba, which is the Hebrew word for daddy (Romans 8:15).

Every day since this encounter, I have run to my armchair which I imagine is my Daddy God's arms. I wake each day and rest on his chest to hear his heart for me and the world. That is the place that I pray and make decrees from. That is where I am healed from my hurts, where I take trips to heaven and where I get wisdom for my life and ministry. This relationship with the Father is vital for every believer to have in order to know what is fully available to them as co-heirs with Christ. Fathers impart identity to their children. But we must know who he is so we can see who we are in his image. Everything I am walking in today has all been birthed from this intimacy with my friend and my Father.

Now, you might be thinking, "I had the best earthly father a person could ask for, so I don't have any daddy issues." To be honest I have a great dad too. Or you may think, "My father was so terrible or so absent I don't even know what a good father looks like." Regardless of where your earthly father falls on the spectrum of good, bad, or absent, you will find so much healing and comfort through this devotional. In fact, if you struggle using a word as intimate as "Daddy" in reference to God, then I KNOW you are in for a breakthrough! Truth be told, even the best earthly father is still only human, which means that all of us in one way or another, need a revelation of being loved by a perfect father, which is God. Let me tell you, he is so much better than you think he is!

I am not here to point out the flaws of our fathers. What I am here to do with this devotional is to lead you into an intimate encounter with a perfect Heavenly Father who, despite the lies and misunderstandings so many of his children believe about him, is the epitome of kindness, love, and safety for those who belong to him through their faith in Christ. Scripture says that God's ways are "perfect" (Psalm 18:30), and that he is a "faithful God who does no wrong," and is "upright and just" (Deuteronomy 32:4). That makes him the perfect Father you never had. If you didn't have a father who was safe, present, approachable, loving, and had your very best in mind, God – as your Happy Heavenly Father – is waiting to more than make up for what you never had. His goodness and mercy have been chasing you down like a father chases down his running toddler in a crowded supermarket! He has brought you to this very place right here, right now, with eager anticipation to sweep you up in his everlasting arms and press you to his heart that literally beats for you.

Like most prophets, my life is a prophetic parable. My existence is due to the reckless pursuit of a loving father on a rescue mission to get back his lost family. Likewise, this book exists due to the reckless pursuit of our heavenly Father, whose loving arms will never let you go. As you read this book, I pray that you will have the same encounter with the wild love that wrecks your religion and that you come to know your happy Daddy God who keeps you in his Unbreakable Embrace.

RECOMENDATIONS

This is a list of some wonderful authors and books that have greatly influenced my personal heart healing journey with the Father that I highly recommend.

The Father's Embrace by Jack Frost
The Supernatural Ways of Royalty by Kris Vallotton
Exposing the Rejection Mindset by Mark DeJesus
God is Good by Bill Johnson
Loving Your Kids on Purpose by Danny Silk
Called to Reign by Leif Hetland
Becoming Who You Are by Dutch Sheets

HOW TO USE

Each day of this devotional the Lord introduces himself speaking with, "Jehovah Shammah" followed by a prophetic word straight from his heart to yours. The meaning of Jehovah is "Lord" and is derived from the Hebrew word havah meaning "to be" or "to exist." It also suggests "to become known" – this denotes a God who desires to reveal himself unceasingly to his children. Shammah is derived from the Hebrew word sham, which can be translated as "there." Jehovah Shammah literally means, "the Lord is there to become known". I have included this so that when you start your devotional, you will immediately hear the Lord say, "Your Daddy is here," followed by his loving words that will demolish the lies that have made you feel unworthy, unseen, unloved, or unwanted. Be at peace; Daddy is here, and he desires to be known by you.

To receive the most dramatic impact out of this devotional, you will want to reserve at least thirty minutes each morning to sit with the Lord. Find a cozy place, without distractions and turn on some Christian soaking music. A few artists on YouTube I suggest are, Eric Gilmore, William Augusto and Julie True. I also highly recommend Return to Eden: The Unveiling on iTunes.

Be sure to search your heart for any bitterness or unforgiveness toward yourself or others. Jesus said in Luke 6:35-37 "Rather love your enemies and continue to treat them well.... you will be known as true children of the Most High God, having his same nature. Be like your Father who is famous for his kindness to heal even the thankless and cruel. Overflow with mercy and compassion for others, just as your heavenly Father overflows with mercy and compassion for all... Forsake the habit of criticizing and judging others, and you will not be criticized and judged in return. Don't condemn others and you will not be condemned. Forgive over and over, and you will be forgiven over and over." Another passage states that not only will God not forgive our sins if we refuse to forgive others, but that our prayers will be hindered because of our unforgiveness (1 Peter 3:7). Forgiveness is not saying that what the person who harmed us did was okay; it is saying that what they did to us longer has a legal right to control and hinder our lives. Jesus took all our sin, including sin against us, to the cross (1 Peter 2:24). He paid for it all so we could be free to live an abundant life free from sin INCLUDING the sin that was committed against us! We are not victims any longer, we are victorious through Christ. As royal sons and daughters of God we have power now to release those who sinned against us because the Father displayed his love by sending his Son to die for us while we were still sinners (Romans 5:8). Be powerful! In the words of another famous princess I know, "Let it go, let it go!"

When you are finally settled in and have your heart right before God, take some time to just worship him. When we worship, we are kissing the face of God. Thank him for whatever comes to mind and release any burdens that might be distracting you. Praise and thanksgiving are the keys that open the gate to your Father's throne room. When you read the prophetic word from the Father, I suggest that you read it out loud to yourself. Call on the name Jehovah Shammah, your Father who is there with you, and feel his presence as you recognize he is there to be found by you.

The Bible says that faith comes by hearing the word of God, (Romans 10:17). I have discovered that, not only does my faith grow when I hear with my natural ears what God is saying, but I can tangibly feel his manifest presence on my physical body. Just like the heaviness of my dad's arms on my shoulders, giving me a warm hug. Doesn't that sound so nice? Isn't that why you are here? An encounter with the Father's love is definitely worth reading out loud for!

After each prophetic word from the Father, you will find a simple prayer in response to what He said. I also suggest that you read this out loud. Building a relationship with another person requires interaction. The purpose of the prayer is to help you engage in a heartfelt conversation with your Father God.

no longer has a legal right to control and hinder our lives. Jesus took all our sin, including sin against us, to the cross (1 Peter 2:24). He paid for it all so we could be free to live an abundant life free from sin INCLUDING the sin that was committed against us! We are not victims any longer, we are victorious through Christ. As royal sons and daughters of God we have power now to release those who sinned against us because the Father displayed his love by sending his Son to die for us while we were still sinners (Romans 5:8). Be powerful! In the words of another famous princess I know, "Let it go, let it go!"

When you are finally settled in and have your heart right before God, take some time to just worship him. When we worship, we are kissing the face of God. Thank him for whatever comes to mind and release any burdens that might be distracting you. Praise and thanksgiving are the keys that open the gate to your Father's throne room. When you read the prophetic word from the Father, I suggest that you read it out loud to yourself. Call on the name Jehovah Shammah, your Father who is there with you, and feel his presence as you recognize he is there to be found by you.

The Bible says that faith comes by hearing the word of God, (Romans 10:17). I have discovered that, not only does my faith grow when I hear with my natural ears what God is saying, but I can tangibly feel his manifest presence on my physical body. Just like the heaviness of my dad's arms on my shoulders, giving me a warm hug. Doesn't that sound so nice? Isn't that why you are here? An encounter with the Father's love is definitely worth reading out loud for!

After each prophetic word from the Father, you will find a simple prayer in response to what He said. I also suggest that you read this out loud. Building a relationship with another person requires interaction. The purpose of the prayer is to help you engage in a heartfelt conversation with your Father God.

The "Selah" section is my favorite. The word Selah in Hebrew means to pause, reflect, wait, or praise. It's often described as a moment of tension between wrestling within our own soul and waiting on God's answer. King David knew all about Selah! When we read many of his psalms, we see him pour his heart out in anguish to the Lord one minute, and then after the Selah, David is praising and worshiping the Lord for his goodness! This is not because David was bipolar. He wasn't; although it would appear that way if you didn't know what David was actually doing during Selah. The Selah is the space where David gives God room to pour his own heart out onto David in response. I have included the practice of Selah with each devotion so that, like King David, you can invite the Father to speak to you. This is where you will find space to journal what you receive in personal ministry directly from him straight to your heart.

If you feel like you don't know how to hear God speak, don't worry. It's not complicated, and it won't come by trying harder to listen, but by simply resting in his love and trusting in his desire to want to talk to you more than you want to hear him! He already gave Jesus for you, how much more will he give you if he didn't even withhold his only Son? His voice is not always a shout, or even a whisper from the outside of us. Although he does speak audibly at times, most of the time it is a still, small voice on the inside of us, because that's where he lives, we are his temple (Hebrews 3:1-6). Since he lives in us, and we have the mind of Christ, and can receive what he perceives (1 Corinthians 2:16), his voice will seem a lot like our own thoughts and feelings. He might come communicate in a gentle thought that pops in your head, or in a picture that flashes across your imagination. It might be a scripture that comes to mind or even an inner knowing, like a gut feeling or a hunch. Take time in the stillness to listen for what he may be speaking. If you feel like you are struggling to experience his communication with you, here are two verses spoken by God, himself, for you to meditate on:

"Then you will call on Me and you will come and pray to Me, and I will hear [your voice] and I will listen to you. Then [with a deep longing] you will seek Me and require Me [as a vital necessity] and [you will] find Me when you search for Me with all your heart."
Jeremiah 29:12-13 AMP

"Call to me and I will answer you and tell you [and even show you] great and mighty things, [things which have been confined and hidden], which you do not know."
Jeremiah 33:3 AMP

Finally, we come to the "Decree" section! If you were thinking you were going to get out of reading out loud here, I hate to disappoint you, but you're wrong. I know it may give you flashbacks to that awkward reading circle time in fifth grade language arts class, but just like good ol' Mrs. Abrams used to say, "I promise, you will thank me later!"

Job 22:28 says that you "shall decree a thing and it shall be established." The English definition of decree is "a statement of truth that carries the authority of a court order". In Latin, decree can also mean "to decide," while the Hebrew meaning can be, "cut off." All that to say, when you are making these decrees from your position as a royal king priest and child of God, you are deciding to believe and bring into your life a statement of truth that carries the authority of heavens courts in order to cut off the influence of demons, past trauma and all the lies you have ever believed about who you are and who God is to you! Now that is kicking the devil right in his ugly teeth, don't you think? Not to mention that whole thing I mentioned before about "faith comes by hearing." Selah, on that for a moment! Powerful!

Of course, you are free to engage as much or as little as you would like with these suggestions. If you miss a day or two, no worries, pick up where you left off. If there is one specific devotional that you need to spend extra time on to get it to sink into your heart, then do it! This is not a race to get to God - it is a journey WITH God! Your breakthrough in getting rid of the things that make you feel far from God isn't going to come because of how diligent you are to start and finish this devotional in 40-days. It's in discovering that after you sit this book down, the God of the breakthrough goes with you and never leaves you! I bless you to receive as much as possible through this 40-day journey to discover Daddy God. He has so much to share with you and has been looking forward to this since you were just a twinkle in his eye way back before the foundation of the earth was laid. I pray that even now you would be baptized in the Father's love! That you would feel the heavens open, see the Holy Spirit descend on you and that you would hear the voice of your Father say, "You are my beloved child that makes me happy!" In Jesus name and for his glory! Amen

Jehovah Shammah Daddy is here

DAY 1

So often you feel alone Beloved, but separation from me is an illusion. There is nowhere you can go to outrun my presence. My goodness, my mercy, and my love are continually chasing you down. Like a Good Father chases his running child so am I chasing after your heart and affections today, My Child. Take time this morning to cease your racing thoughts. Surrender your to-do list to me and I will show you the best path to take today. Let me take your burdens like a sack upon my shoulder. Let me take you up into my everlasting arms that never tire of holding you close to my heart. Feel my heartbeat for you as you rest against my chest. Breathe deep my Spirit around you and exhale your worries. Know that as you embark on your day today that my love will not let you down, my love is incapable of failing you. Don't be obsessed with what you lack but live content with what you have, for you always have My presence. I promise you, I will never leave you alone, never! And I will not loosen my grip on your life! You are safe here in my unbreakable embrace.

Love,
Your Happy Daddy God

Prayer

Abba, thank you for your presence in my life. Teach me to turn into your love for me quickly and not run in endless cycles of busyness. Give me grace to stay in awareness of your nearness to me today. I renounce the lie that I am alone when I can't feel you with me. I receive your love for me today and I ask that you teach me to know you and love you more and to love the world around me the same way you love me. I thank you for the ability to live from your heart today. In Jesus' name, amen.

Selah
Pause • Wait • Meditate • Listen

Look with wonder at the depth of the Father's marvelous love that he has lavished on us! He has called us and made us his very own beloved children. The reason the world doesn't recognize who we are is that they didn't recognize him. 1 John 3:1 TPT

Decree

I decree that my spiritual senses are in tune with heaven, and I easily perceive, receive, and release communication with the Lord.

I decree that my lips will continually praise the Lord with hymns and psalms and spontaneous songs sung in the spirit.

I decree I am not a worrier; I am a worshipper!

I decree everything I do is an act of worship because I do it all in fellowship with the Lord and for God's glory.

I decree God made me to be a unique instrument of worship. I will not compare my worship to others.

I decree I find unique, creative expressions to worship God through song, dance and other art forms and he loves it!

I decree when the world overwhelms me with the cares of life, worship becomes the path of ascension into the presence of God.

I decree when I praise him, The Lord fights my battles

Jehovah Shammah Daddy is here

DAY 2

Good morning, beautiful one! Can you hear the sound around you this new day? Pause and listen — the coo of a newborn child, the birds always chirping, the trees rustling, the wind whistling, the rivers and streams babbling, the ocean crashing in rhythmic percussion... all in a symphony of worship to me. All creation acts as my orchestra as I sing my love song over you. Every love song ever written by man could never hold a flame next to the one I wrote just for you. Through Jesus, you have been invited back into the dance with us. Rejoice in our relationship today and let my spirit lead you as a skilled dance partner would. It's okay if you stumble as you learn. I am not easily offended, and you can't step on my toes. Regroup in my arms and try again. Focus your heart on me and release your affection in psalms and hymns and spontaneous spiritual songs. Your worship arrests my heart and captures my gaze. My eyes search to find my laid-down lovers who worship me in spirit and in truth. When you worship, you transcend the worries of the world, and you can see that I am constantly dancing and singing over you with gladness!

Love, Daddy God who sings over you

Prayer

Abba, thank you that through the blood of Jesus I have come back into fellowship with the Trinity! How wonderful to be the theme of your love song! Teach me to be surrendered and led by Holy Spirit today. Fill me with passionate praise so that the world may know your wonderful deeds! Today is the day that you have made, so I will rejoice and be glad in it, as you are glad about me! In Jesus name. Amen!

Selah
Pause • Wait • Meditate • Listen

Look with wonder at the depth of the Father's marvelous love that he has lavished on us! He has called us and made us his very own beloved children. The reason the world doesn't recognize who we are is that they didn't recognize him. 1 John 3:1 TPT

Decree

I decree that my spiritual senses are in tune with heaven, and I easily perceive, receive, and release communication with the Lord.

I decree that my lips will continually praise the Lord with hymns and psalms and spontaneous songs sung in the spirit.

I decree I am not a worrier; I am a worshipper!

I decree everything I do is an act of worship because I do it all in fellowship with the Lord and for God's glory.

I decree God made me to be a unique instrument of worship. I will not compare my worship to others.

I decree I find unique, creative expressions to worship God through song, dance and other art forms and he loves it!

I decree when the world overwhelms me with the cares of life, worship becomes the path of ascension into the presence of God.

I decree when I praise him, The Lord fights my battles

Jehovah Shammah Daddy is here

DAY 3

Come away with me, my Love, it's a new day and I have good plans for you! As you spend time with me this morning, I invite you to drink deep the river of bliss that flows from my heart into yours. Every dry place in your soul will be drenched by my delight as you worship me. I am your oasis in a parched and weary land. So, drink of my love for you, as I drink you in. Your love satisfies me as I know I am the only thing that satisfies the deep need in you. You were made for this, to be the object of my affection and to love me in return. Your high calling is not that of apostle, prophet, evangelist, pastor or teacher, no. It is to be MY BELOVED CHILD and you have my permission to be intoxicated by my love for you. The ministry of Jesus began with turning water into wine at the wedding at Canna and was punctuated at the last supper with wine in Holy Communion. Now by grace through faith you can enjoy the pleasure of union with my spirit living richly within you and bubbling up into eternal life. What is in me is also in you. As you are freshly filled with my spirit, morning by morning, you become a vessel of overflow, spilling my glory and goodness out about and around you everywhere you go. I bless you to live from the overflow. Love, Daddy God who is proud of you

Prayer

.

Jesus, you are certainly my living water and the one true source of life, love and satisfaction for every human soul! Lord I confess I need you to refresh me by your spirit! I want to experience the bliss of your nature in fullness dwelling in me. Like a deer pants for the water, so my soul thirsts for you. Please fill me afresh until I am overflowing with you. In Jesus name. Amen

Selah
Pause • Wait • Meditate • Listen

I overflow with praise when I come before you, for the anointing of your presence satisfies me like nothing else. You are such a rich banquet of pleasure to my soul. Psalms 63:5 TPT

Decree

I decree that I enjoy the fountain of delight that springs up from my spirit in union with Christ.
I decree that I overflow with the spirit of God that turns dry wastelands into beautiful gardens.
I decree where I go, God goes. Where he is, there is life. I will release his life from within me everywhere we go today.
I decree I am free to be captured by the bliss of my life union with my Jesus.
I decree God's love is sweeter than the finest wine and by faith I receive the joy of being one with him.
I decree that every addiction and counterfeit for the Holy Spirit must be broke off me, now, in Jesus' name.
I decree God's supply never runs out. I can have as much of him as I want, and he will not withhold himself from me.
I decree when I invite him, Jesus makes even the most mundane and menial tasks a pleasure just because he is there.
I decree I can be transported to his house of wine whenever I am willing to linger with him in worship

Jehovah Shammah Daddy is here

DAY 4

Turn your heart and eyes on me today, beloved, not on what the enemy is doing! Just as when Peter stepped out of the boat and was able to walk on the water when he looked at me but then, turning his eyes to the storm, he began to drown. Refuse to focus on the storm. Do you not remember that I am the same God that commands the storm to be at peace and be still? Guard your eyes, your ears, and your mouth from evil. Look at me, my eyes never depart from my lovers; neither do I slumber or sleep. I am always watching over you. My angels are on assignment to watch over you. Focus on my love for you and then focus on what I love in the people I have given you. What you focus on is what you will manifest and magnify. True prophecy is the testimony of how Jesus loves humanity. When you focus on whatever is lovely, noble, and praiseworthy, you will see more love, more nobility and have more reason to praise! Speak life, not death, love and not hate, unity and not division, humility and not pride. Call forth the treasure hidden in the messy people and situations around you, and you will prophesy my heart over it all today my love.

Love, Daddy God who protects you

Prayer

Father, thank you for the authority you have given me through your Son Jesus! I renounce and tear down any word curses I have spoken over my life or over the lives of others. I decree blessings instead of curses and I ask for your grace to help me know when to speak and what to speak so that I might choose life and build your kingdom by word and deed. In Jesus name. Amen

Selah

Pause • Wait • Meditate • Listen

"The Lord sees all we do; he watches over his friends, day and night. His godly ones receive the answers they seek whenever they cry out to him." Psalms 34:15 TPT

Decree

I decree that my attention is focused on heavenly realities and when I speak, resurrection power goes out and makes dead things come to life.

I decree I have eyes that are sensitive to see what my Heavenly Father sees and speaks.

I decree I consistently see the treasure hidden within others, even the most difficult people I have a grace to see them for who God made them to be and I call that out of them.

I decree that I am slow to speak and quick to listen. I am wise with my words, and I know when to speak up and when to stay silent.

I decree every assignment of distraction be broken off me, in Jesus' name.

I decree God always speaks through me to comfort, encourage, and build up others when they need it most

Jehovah Shammah Daddy is here

DAY 5

Your body is important to me, but it was given to serve you, not for you to serve it. Do you remember how the children of Israel forgot so quickly of the burden of their slavery and the mighty miracles I performed to bring them out of their bondage? My heart was broken as they grumbled against me and lusted for the meat pots of Egypt. They did not know it, but they worshipped worldly comfort, rejecting relationship with me who wanted to be their comforter. You have a better covenant by the blood of Jesus than they did. Now my word is inscribed upon your heart and my spirit lives on the inside of you to give you power to subdue your flesh and live from my eternal life. I have not promised that your life in the flesh will be comfortable. In fact, your flesh is at enmity with the spirit and will frequently be challenged with discomfort. I did not make you to be a slave to your flesh. My Spirit within you is training you to bring your flesh into the subjection of the life of Spirit. In Christ you have died to the life of the flesh and discomfort is an indicator that my Spirit is showing you an area of your heart that still needs to come into subjection to the life of the Spirit. Take heart knowing that this momentary and light affliction is producing in you a greater weight of glory.
Love, Daddy God who soothes your soul

Prayer

Father thank you for your mercy that is new each morning. Search me and know me and reveal any wicked way in me. I repent for any way I have made carnal comforts an idol and for operating in the lust of the flesh, the lust of the eyes and the pride of life. I receive you as my comforter. I welcome the life of your Spirit in me to continually reveal any area where my old flesh nature tries to resurface, so that I can swiftly put it to death and know the power of your resurrection life working within me. In Jesus name, Amen.

Selah

Pause • Wait • Meditate • Listen

"Live as one who has died to every form of sexual sin and impurity. Live as one who has died to the desires for forbidden things, including the desire for wealth, which is the essence of idol worship." Colossians 3:5 TPT

Decree

I decree that I recognize the schemes of the enemy and he will not trick me into going back to my old way of life.
I decree that my soul and flesh are in subjection to my spirit man.
I decree that I welcome challenges as opportunities to grow in my faith knowing that I am being perfected in his likeness.
I decree that I will not have eyes for other gods, or lesser lovers than Jesus.
I decree Jesus is the love of my life because I am the love of his.
I decree that I do not have to settle for a counterfeit comforter when I have the Comforter, Holy Spirit.
I decree Holy Spirit is constantly with me pouring life and strength into me when I am nestled securely in his arms

Jehovah Shammah Daddy is here

DAY 6

My darling, today I desire for you to live from the security that you are fully known and fully loved by me. I know every one of your thoughts before you think them. I know what you will say before you speak. I know everything about you, and I still love you. Just one look from your worshipping eyes ravishes my heart. Don't allow shame and fear to cause you to hide from me. When you stumble know that I saw your stumbling from afar off and I was always standing by to catch you. Let me love on you and tell you who you really are in me. I have given you my righteousness and my grace to keep you from falling and staying down. So, arise, my beloved, dust disappointment off and let's enjoy this beautiful new day together! Love, Daddy God who holds your hand

Prayer

Father, thank you for your grace and your forgiveness when I fall short of your perfection. Your radical love makes me desire to know you more and be more like you. Help me to comprehend the depths of your love so that I can become your love to the lost and hurting world around me. Convict me when I step outside of my born again nature as your child. In your goodness lead me away from temptation and all self-centeredness. I want to be just like you, my Daddy God. In Jesus name. Amen.

Selah
Pause • Wait • Meditate • Listen

"You've gone into my future to prepare the way, and in kindness you follow behind me to spare me from the harm of my past. You have laid your hand on me! This is just too wonderful, deep, and incomprehensible! Your understanding of me brings me wonder and strength." Psalms 139:5-6 TPT

Decree

I decree that I am already completely known and completely loved by God. There is nothing I can do to earn his approval. His accepting love is the free gift.

I decree that I am the righteousness of God in Christ Jesus and although I may stumble, I don't stay down.

I decree I get up and I will shake off disappointment quickly because Holy Spirit has made me an overcomer.

I decree I am not the sum of my past mistakes. I am a brand new creation in Jesus.

I decree the old me is dead and gone and the life I live now is a new life in Christ.

I decree I quickly learn from my mistakes so that I can be who the Father says I am the next time I make a mistake.

I decree that each day I am learning more and more how to walk in love, like Jesus did, because love fulfills all the law and commandments.

I decree there is no condemnation for me in Christ!

I decree conviction is the Father's nature in me calling me to be who he created me to be, it is not to shame me, but to call me up to where I belong.

I decree when my heart and mind condemn me, I will run to God, not away from him, knowing I can receive grace in my time of need.

Jehovah Shammah Daddy is here

DAY 7

The first thing the enemy does is try to get you to forget who you are and who you belong to. He will get you to agree with his lies to burden you and weigh you down until you believe you are defeated. Come to me and rejoice in our relationship and I will shake off the lies, the shame, and the heaviness. I believe in you because I believe in the Spirit I put in you, my own Spirit. You are not identified by your shortcomings or by the opinions of man. You are identified by the blood of my Son and now we dance and sing over you with great joy. So, face me and prepare to let me lead. Put your hands in mine and look into my eyes without fear. When I look into your eyes, I see myself in them. As you look at me you reflect what you see. You are safe to rest your head on my chest and be swept up by the pounding of my heartbeat that echoes your name. My heart is always calling out to you, dear. As you tune into my heart you know which steps to take, and your life will be an absolute ball! Now give this message to your brothers and sisters. I want to dance with them too. You can trust that I will not let you down like other people have. I am a good Father, and I am in a good mood over you consistently.
Love, Daddy God who dances with you

Prayer

Father, forgive me for believing lies about myself and my value. I renounce all the lies sent by the enemy to steal your unique expression through me in my generation. I am so thankful for a God who reminds me that I am his dearly beloved child. I confess that I am who you say I am. Teach me to see the power of your spirit living on the inside of me so that when the enemy tries to wear me out and tear me down I will be quick to take every thought captive and force it to come into obedience to your thoughts. In Jesus name. Amen.

Pause • Wait • Meditate • Listen

""The Lord your God is in your midst, A Warrior who saves. He will rejoice over you with joy; he will be quiet in His love [making no mention of your past sins], he will rejoice over you with shouts of joy." Zephaniah 3:17 AMP

Decree

I decree I am led by the Holy Spirit.
I decree God is a happy Father who dances and sings over me with joy!
I decree the joy of the Lord is my strength.
I decree I recognize lies from the enemy and laugh at them just like my Father God sits in heaven and laughs at his enemies.
I decree I have what it takes to accomplish every good thing the Lord created me for.
I decree those ungodly burdens and heaviness must leave my life, now, in Jesus' name. I receive beauty for ashes and put on a new garment of praise!
I decree that seriousness is not a fruit of the Spirit, but joy is, and I experience overwhelming joy when I meditate on God's love and joy in me.
I decree that when I pray for people they are delivered and healed from mental and emotional illnesses by Jesus on the spot.
I decree I have been anointed with the oil of joy for mourning and people recognize this about me

Jehovah Shammah Daddy is here

DAY 8

In your brokenness I found you and purchased you with immense delight. I took you and wrapped you up with my robe of righteousness and brought you home with me to my Father's house. I hold you in my nail pierced hands. My loving eyes look over every part of you with joy. I know the treasure I have found. Let the warmth of my healing hands seep deep into your soul and bring you peace. Meditate on my word and it will wash you like pure sparkling water. As you spend time in the water of my word it will wash away all the dirt and impurities from your years of brokenness. Do not fear, I am meek and mild and gentle around your fractured edges. I came to heal the broken hearted and bind their wounds. With perfect precision I will fill your fractured pieces with my love like pure gold. As you glory in my presence you will be filled with my Spirit until you overflow. Your cup will run over with my goodness, and you will satisfy the thirsty ones with the story of my redeeming love that saved you and made you whole! Trust the process, precious one! I am preparing you to be a vessel of honor made for the good work of the Master. I delight in you and all that you are becoming.

Love, Daddy God who rescues you

Prayer

Jesus, when I think about how you rescued me from darkness, I am undone by your love! Today I give you all my fractured and jagged edges and I trust you in this process of making me whole. Have your way in my life, Lord, so that I can be used for your glory. In Jesus name. Amen!

Selah
Pause • Wait • Meditate • Listen

"Then, looking into Thomas' eyes, he said, "Put your finger here in the wounds of my hands. Here—put your hand into my wounded side and see for yourself. Thomas, don't give in to your doubts any longer, just believe!" John 20:27 TPT

Decree

I decree that I shall recover all that the enemy stole from me according to the blood of Jesus who died for me.

I decree that I have a spirit of revelation and wisdom to read and comprehend the written word of God.

I decree that I discover fresh insights in scripture daily, and I get excited as I seek them out.

I decree that by the stripes of Jesus I am healed, saved, delivered, and made whole!

I decree that I have the mind of Christ.

I decree that I live from the overflow of God's Spirit.

I decree I have an incredible ability to meditate on God's promises in scripture, especially when the enemy tries to attack me with worry.

I decree that my thoughts are focused on God so I am full of peace.

I decree that every spirit of drama and distraction must be broken off of my life now in Jesus name.

I decree that every hook and snare of chaos must be shattered in the name of Jesus and replaced with the perfect peace of God.

Jehovah Shammah Daddy is here

DAY 9

You stand locked in my everlasting embrace, beloved. Lean into my love and feel my arms are wrapped around you holding you securely no matter what you face. Here your fears are arrested, and my uncompromising, unconditional love washes over you like a waterfall. My waves of love engulf you and take you over. You are swept up in my love; captured in heavens embrace. All the dryness from the wilderness season is quickly flooded by my love and mercy. I am the Living Water and the one your soul longs for. Your worship is like sweet water to me. I love the moments when we drink each other in. I am satisfied with your love as you are satisfied in mine. As you are refreshed by my love, I will make every barren wasteland become an oasis of delight. Once you have had your fill you will be like an overflowing cup, splashing my presence on everyone around you. I bless you to be love drunk on me today and introduce my Spirit to a multitude of thirsty souls that they may drink their fill and share eternal life with us.
Love, Daddy God who satisfies you

Prayer

Lord, thank you for being my refuge and my strength. When I am dissatisfied, keep me from the evil of trying to find my satisfaction anywhere but in your presence. Forgive me for the times I have ran from you when I should have ran to you. You are my wellspring of life, and the water of your precious Holy Spirit restores and refreshes my soul. Today I will live saturated by your love and kindness, Father. In Jesus name. Amen

Selah

Pause • Wait • Meditate • Listen

Jesus answered, "If you drink from Jacob's well, you'll be thirsty again and again, but if anyone drinks the living water I give them, they will never thirst again and will be forever satisfied! For when you drink the water, I give you it becomes a gushing fountain of the Holy Spirit, springing up and flooding you with endless life!" John 4:13-14 TP

Decree

I decree the life of Christ in me is a gushing fountain of living water springing up and flooding me with endless life!
I decree Jesus satisfies my life by his Holy Spirit.
I decree there is an oasis of righteousness, peace, and joy within me.
I decree God's Spirit is empowering me to do in his strength what would be impossible in my own strength.
I decree the Holy Spirit is a gushing fountain of life that bubbles up within me and overflows out of me splashing others who need to be refreshed by it.
I decree ideas, inspiration, heavenly wisdom, and supernatural abilities bubble up and out of me.
I decree I am an uncapped well of revival.
I decree I am a heavy drinker in the Spirit. As I worship God in spirit and in truth, I am drinking from Christ who is my cup of bliss, as I am his.

Jehovah Shammah Daddy is here

DAY 10

Darling, slow down and rest your mind on me before you start your day. I see your racing thoughts, your endless to-do list. Surrender it all to me, my love. I know what you need to accomplish today, but first let me hold you. Let me love on you and infuse you with strength. As you surrender your time to me, I will expand time for you. Whatever you sow, you will also reap. Sow a tithe of your time to me each morning and watch as I multiply time for you to accomplish all that is required for you to do and more. I will redeem your time and restore the years the locust devoured. As you make meeting time with me a priority, I will meet all your needs for time and more. I will give you peace to subdue the days chaos. I will give you wisdom and understanding to lead your life efficiently and effectively for your kingdom assignment. I will orchestrate divine appointments and my Spirit will help you be in my perfect timing. This way you will never be late for I am always right on time!
Love, Daddy God who makes time for you

Prayer

Father, thank you for this reminder to spend time with you each day! It is a joy and a delight to be desired by you! I love our time together. Help me be guided by your timing and to not get too far ahead of you or to lag behind. Teach me to understand the brevity of life and to live each day for your glory. In Jesus name. Amen

Selah
Pause • Wait • Meditate • Listen

"So be very careful how you live, not being like those with no understanding, but live honorably with true wisdom, for we are living in evil times. Take full advantage of every day as you spend your life for his purposes." Ephesians 5:15-16 TPT

Decree

I decree the spirit of delay is broken off my life, in Jesus' name.
I decree the Lord is restoring and redeeming my time as I surrender my time to his loving care.
I decree I am always on time because I serve an on-time God.
I decree I am anointed to know the times and the seasons.
I decree I manage time well to accomplish my kingdom purposes.
I decree I am always in the right place at the right time because my footsteps are ordered by the Lord.
I decree time miracles happen frequently around me.
I decree I will not miss my appointed time.
I decree I was made for a time such as this.
I decree I am not hindered by time, but God is releasing rapid acceleration for me to accomplish in little time what would have taken a long time

Jehovah Shammah Daddy is here

DAY 11

Come sit on my lap this morning and let me tell you who you are to me. The world around you will try and tell you that your identity is in your past mistakes, your struggles, your preferences or even the in the things you do. These are all lies. Any identity not rooted in your new creation through Christ is a false identity. Your job does not define you. Your sin and shortcomings do not define you. You are not the sum of your weaknesses. Your value is not dictated by the people who have wronged you. You exist for this reason: to be loved by me and to be a reflection of my love to the world around you. You are who I say you are. Let my word about your identity be enough. You are my beloved. I proved your value by sending my Son to the cross, a life in exchange for a life. The same love I have for my Son, Jesus, I also have for you. It was always my plan to love you. In fact, I loved you before you ever existed because I knew you and loved you before time began. So, discard all the lies and take in this reality: You are the love of my life and the cross proved it. You were created to be the object of my affection. You were made for love; to be loved by me and then to become love to those around you. No need to search any longer for who you are. Just let me love you and everything else will flow from that reality.
Love, Daddy God who wants you

Prayer

Father, some days it is so easy for me to forget how much you love me. I acknowledge that my value is not in what I do for you or what others think of me, but my value was determined by the high price Jesus paid for me. Give me grace to receive my identity fully in who your word says I am in Christ, a dearly beloved child of God! In Jesus name. Amen!

Selah
Pause • Wait • Meditate • Listen

"We look away from the natural realm and we focus our attention and expectation onto Jesus who birthed faith within us and who leads us forward into faith's perfection. His example is this: Because his heart was focused on the joy of knowing that you would be his, he endured the agony of the cross and conquered its humiliation, and now sits exalted at the right hand of the throne of God!" Hebrews 12:2 TPT

Decree

I decree I renounce self-rejection and self-hatred in Jesus' name. I take back all authority I submitted to rejection and hatred, and I cast it out of my life now in Jesus' name.

I decree my Father God thinks I am beautiful, and I believe it.

I decree I am beautiful inside, and out, because I look like my Father God who made me in his image.

I decree I love and care for my body because it is God's house.

I decree I am fearfully and wonderfully made by a loving Creator God who does not make mistakes.

I decree that as I experience God's love for me, I am learning how to love and like myself in the same way.

I decree I renounce every false identity and orphan mindset.

I decree I am not a slave to fear, sin or the opinions of people.

I decree I am free to love and serve God.

I decree that I am extravagantly loved by an amazing Father God who takes delight in me and predestined me to be his.

Jehovah Shammah Daddy is here

DAY 12

I have smiling eyes over you. There are so many of my precious children that have believed that I have taken my eyes off them because I am displeased, but this is a lie. My eyes are always on you and my countenance is shining on you day and night. I am a happy Daddy. I will never yell at you or strike you. Jesus received the punishment for your sin so that you could be reconciled back to my royal family! The consequences of sin are punishment enough which is why I have given my sons and daughters the same grace that Jesus had to overcome sin by living surrendered to my Spirit in them. You are no longer a sinner in my eyes. Come be with me and let me teach you how to be free from the things that try to ensnare you. I am not an abusive father. Let me show you who you really are and all that you now possess as my child. I am a happy Daddy that shouted over you, "This is my dearly beloved child in whom I am well pleased!" the very moment you first believed on my Son and became born again into my kingdom! Have peace knowing this: I will never change my mind about you.

Love, Daddy God who pays attention to you

Prayer

Father, you are so wonderful. You are so much more kind than I sometimes believe. Get rid of any doubt I have in your goodness. Fill me with faith to know and believe that you are pleased with me. Empower me by your Spirit to live in sweet surrender to your life inside of me. Thank you for never changing your mind about loving me! In Jesus name. Amen!

🎁 **A gift for you**

Enjoy your gift! From Mom

amazon Gift Receipt

Send a Thank You Note
You can learn more about your gift or start a return here too.

Scan using the Amazon app or visit
https://a.co/d/edU5FVr

Unbreakable Embrace A 40 Day Devotional with Decrees: Destroy The Separation Mindset And Dive Into The Arms Of A Happy D...
Order ID: 113-0301172-9771440 Ordered on February 9, 2022

"Yahweh looks down in love, looking over all of Adam's sons and daughters. He's looking to see if there is anyone who acts wisely, any who are searching for God and wanting to please him." Psalms 14:2 TPT

Decree

I decree God sees me, God knows me, God likes me, and God loves me.

I decree that the spirit of condemnation and fear of punishment is broken off my life, now, in Jesus' name.

I decree The Lord never turns his eyes in shame from me, but he is constantly looking with tender hearted love and affection over all the details of my heart, soul, and life.

I decree I am no longer a sinner; I am a new creation in Christ and sin is not part of my identity in him.

I decree I am full of confidence in God's love for me.

I decree Jesus took my punishment so that I could receive his righteousness.

I decree I am learning to live as a beloved child of God with an increased awareness of being righteous in him.

I decree that as I walk in fellowship with God I am growing in holiness.

Jehovah Shammah Daddy is here

DAY 13

Arise and shine, my love! A new day has dawned over you! Can you feel the freshness in the air around you? Can you feel the tingle of my great expectation resonating in the depths of your soul? You have every reason to celebrate this new day bursting forth around you! Do not let the cares of yesterday weigh you down. Stop living life looking in the rearview mirror. You can't move forward if you keep looking back at the things of the past. Remember Lot's wife who turned to look behind her at the destruction of Sodom and Gomorrah and was turned into a pillar of salt. When you focus on the pain of your past you are frozen from moving into your future. Let it all go — the good, the bad, the ugly, the hurts, the hang ups, the hope deferred — give it all to me. I am writing an entirely new chapter in your life today. The page is blank. Your slate is clean, and my mercies are new every morning. Your new story is written for my glory, and I always finish with a happy ending.
Love, Daddy God who rewrites your story

Prayer

Father today I make a choice to surrender all my past into your loving hands. Thank you for having good plans for my future that I can trust to bring me to a good end full of success and prosperity. I receive your forgiveness and your mercy as I walk into this new day of destiny. In Jesus name. Amen!

Selah
Pause • Wait • Meditate • Listen

"You saw who you created me to be before I became me! Before I'd ever seen the light of day, the number of days you planned for me were already recorded in your book." Psalms 139:16 TPT

Decree

I decree I will not let my past dictate my future.
I decree I will only allow the word and the will of God to dictate and direct my life.
I decree that every false and demonic narrative operating in my life be exposed as a lie and rendered null and void, now, in Jesus' name.
I decree I will rejoice and celebrate the goodness of God as I rapidly advance from this day forward.
I decree I am focusing on the high call of Christ Jesus and going from glory to glory and strength to strength.
I decree I come out of agreement with every word curse spoken over me and I render it null and void, in Jesus' name
I decree my testimony is POWERFUL to destroy satan.
I decree I love to share my testimony with boldness, because the person I was no longer lives but Christ has given me a new life and a clean slate.
I decree when people hear my testimony it creates a realm of hope that others can walk into for God to do what he did for me, for them also.

Jehovah Shammah Daddy is here

DAY 14

Every time you call on my name I come running with a father's help. It is my delight to wrap you up in my presence like a father wraps his arms around his child! My thoughts and intentions toward you are good and more numerous than the sands on the shore or the stars in the cosmos. If I am the God who hung the stars and called them each by name, how could I ever forget you, my precious one? You were my happy thought held and crafted in my holy imagination long before I named the stars! Come today with joy into my presence! I long to be with you! Through the blood of Jesus, you are no longer in trouble. You are truly, madly, deeply, loved by me. I am your Happy Daddy God! Feel the warmth of my shining, smiling face arising over you morning by morning. I have made you more than a conqueror! If I am for you, who then can be against you? Do not fear for I am with you and together we can overcome whatever comes your way.

Love, Daddy God who thinks about you

Prayer

Father, you are my strength and my shield. There is none like you! How wonderful to know I am not alone because I have you. I am amazed to think about how often you think about me! There isn't a detail of my life that you miss. Lord, help me to run to you and not run from you when I do not feel worthy of your love. Continue to help me receive your grace by faith and grow deeper into your joy over me. In Jesus name. Amen!

Selah

Pause • Wait • Meditate • Listen

"The very moment I call to you for a father's help the tide of battle turns and my enemies flee. This one thing I know: God is on my side!" Psalms 56:9 TPT

Decree

I decree I am truly loved by an amazing Father God.

I decree there is no separation between God and me.

I decree God delights in being close to me.

I decree that every spirit of rejection and abandonment must be severed from me, now, in Jesus' name, and they no longer will have any effect on my life.

I decree that the Holy Spirit has full reign over my entire being.

I decree I am not in trouble with God, and every spirit sent to trouble me will fall into its own trap, in Jesus' name.

I decree Holy Spirit is filling up every broken and empty place in my soul until I am overflowing with the fullness of God.

I decree I have my Father God's loving attention. I do not have to beg, throw a fit or overachieve for him to see me.

I decree I have healthy boundaries. I do not need to say "yes" to everything in fear I will disappoint God or people.

I decree I live my life each day from the knowledge that I am enough because Jesus says so.

Jehovah Shammah Daddy is here

DAY 15

I know your thoughts from afar off. I know the inner working of your mind, heart, and intentions. Man might look at your exterior, but I see and know your interior. It is the heart that counts. Did I not come to heal the broken hearted and bind their wounds? Darling, know this about my heart: It is ALWAYS my will to heal. Today invite me into your heartache so that I can heal you. There is no need to hide your real emotions from me. I already know them. Do not hold back in asking me hard questions. Truth is not offended or intimidated when it is questioned. It is always firm and secure. I take joy in providing the answers when you call to me with a humble heart that seeks truth. Count it all joy whenever I allow issues of your heart to be exposed, because what I reveal I always heal. Open your heart to me my love as my heart is open to you. It is safe here and you will find healing as I hold you in my hands that were wounded for you.

Love, Daddy God who heals you

Prayer

Father, thank you for caring about the issues of my heart. I want to have clean hands and a pure heart so that I can see you face to face. I invite you into my heart today to search me and know me. Let me feel your loving presence as you heal me and remove whatever is in me that doesn't look like you. In Jesus name. Amen!

Selah
Pause • Wait • Meditate • Listen

"Jesus reached out his hand and touched the leper and said, 'Of course I want to heal you—be healed!' And instantly, all signs of leprosy disappeared!" Matthew 8:3 TPT

Decree

I decree I am quick to allow God to purify my heart so that I am moved by the impulses of his heart and not those of my flesh.
I decree when the issues of life try to defile my heart, I am quick to forgive and bless those who hurt me.
I decree I will not hide from God when my heart is hurting like Adam and Eve did. I am quick to run to the affirmation of my heavenly Father for the strength and comfort I need.
I decree I have a good heart because Jesus gave me a new one when he moved in.
I decree God is the defender of my heart and it is safe in his hands.
I decree God has anointed me to heal the broken hearted and bind up their wounds.
I decree the spirit of the Lord is upon me to preach good news to the poor and proclaim the year of the Lord's favor and vengeance against his enemies.
I decree I'm not afraid of demons, they are afraid of me, because Christ gave me authority to bind them and send them to the pit to await their final judgment.

Jehovah Shammah Daddy is here

DAY 16

The waiting in the dark has come to an end. Just as a butterfly bursting from its cocoon, "Behold, the old has passed away and all things have become new!" I'm releasing you into the new, to rule and reign in my authority, and it's time to soar on the wind of my Spirit to places you never dreamed you would be able to go! I have given you new eyes to see from my perspective and the battle you overcame in the last season has now given you a higher authority to advance my kingdom in your sphere of influence.

Although the past season was dark, you have come forth, transformed to look more like me, and you are truly a wonder, and beautiful to see! Many people ask for a miracle yet fail to recognize that one of the greatest displays of my resurrection power is the miracle of a transformed life in Christ. Today I put you on display as the miracle you are in me, my beloved. Fly high, rule and reign with me in the higher place!

Love, Daddy God who believes in you

Prayer

Father thank you for never giving up on me! You are so faithful and patient to correct me with your love. Continue to transform me into the image of your Son, Jesus. I want to be a reflection of your transformational power to overcome sin and all the works of darkness. In Jesus name. Amen!

Selah

Pause • Wait • Meditate • Listen

"'You have seen what I did to the Egyptians. You know how I carried you on eagles' wings and brought you to myself."
Exodus 19:4 NLT

Decree

I decree I am the righteousness of God in Christ Jesus.
I decree I am the head, and not the tail. I am above, and not beneath the enemy.
I decree I renounce all agreements I have with the spirit of oppression and depression.
I decree I come out from underneath all spiritual oppression and enemy attacks, and I command them to leave me, and go to the pit now, in Jesus' name.
I decree I have been given authority over the enemy and I trample on serpents and scorpions.
I decree as I behold the beauty of Jesus in prayer and worship, I am becoming more and more like him.
I decree I was made to reflect God's character and nature, and each day I am becoming who God created me to be as I spend time learning who he is.
 I decree I am seated in Christ in heavenly places. I am above all warfare, and all works of darkness are under my feet.

Jehovah Shammah Daddy is here

DAY 17

Look with the eyes of your spirit today. Can you see you are standing on the edge of your Promised Land? Take my hand and we will cross the threshold together, my love. I will carry you into the door of your next season. I won't drop you or let you down. I'll uphold you with my strong arms and give you a good home. Enter my rest and my best for you. This is a good land, flowing with milk and honey! I will satisfy you and give you a super abundant life filled with good things as you trust in my ability to provide and lead you in the best path for your life. The only requirement for you is to forget the former things and lay hold of the new thing I am doing for you. Just as Joshua could not take Moses into the Promised Land, there are certain people, mindsets, and old ways of doing things that you cannot take with you into your new season. This may seem difficult, but it is imperative for your advancement into all I have for you. Lay those things at the foot of the cross and choose to cross over with me into your destiny. Do not fear, be bold and courageous for I will go with you and lead you into all I have promised you for your good and my glory.
Love, Daddy God who opens doors for you

Prayer

Father, as I stand at the edge of each new day, the tasks ahead can feel overwhelming. How wonderful it is to know that I do not need to rely on my strength but only on your Spirit to accomplish everything you have planned for me. God, keep me faithfully moving forward in this life and embolden me to take down every giant that tries to hinder my advancement. In Jesus' name. Amen!

Selah

Pause • Wait • Meditate • Listen

"'Keep trusting in the Lord and do what is right in his eyes. Fix your heart on the promises of God, and you will dwell in the land, feasting on his faithfulness." Psalms 37:3 TPT

Decree

I decree I am strong in the Lord.
I decree I am filled with power and might by the Holy Spirit that lives within me.
I decree Jesus is my promised land and Holy Spirit is the down payment of my heavenly inheritance.
I decree I am continually advancing in my pursuit to know Jesus more intimately.
I decree I am overcoming every hinderance that keeps me from experiencing the full abundant life that Jesus died to give me.
I decree I won't settle for less than what Jesus paid for.
I decree I forget the former things and lay hold of my high calling in Christ Jesus.
I decree today is a new day and God is doing a new thing in my life.
I decree this is the day that the Lord has made, and come what may, I shall rejoice in it!
I decree my praise is a weapon.

Jehovah Shammah Daddy is here

DAY 18

I've set my mark on you. You are the target of my love and affection, and I will not relent until I have all of you. My heart is yours. I hold it out to you, open and vulnerable. Did you know that I, the Son of Man, have a heart of flesh? Yes, there is flesh and bone enthroned at the right hand of your Father in heaven. My heart is tender and compassionate, not cold, and hard. I have placed my heart within you and removed your heart of stone so that you can experience my love for you. My heart is undone by your devoted worship! I am a humble King searching for those who will worship me in spirit and in truth. I am pleased to find a heart of worship in you, my love. Did you know that when you worship you are kissing the very face of God? It is true! Come and taste and see that I am good! You will experience that I really am more than enough for you. Lean into my loving arms when your mind begins to wonder into old places. Turn your thoughts and affectionate praises toward me and you will feel my passion for you rush in like a flood of love. Again, I won't relent until I have all of you. All of me loves all of you and your affection and attention satisfy my heart, as mine satisfies and transforms yours. Come and let us enjoy each other my love, my child, my friend.
Love, Daddy God who is here for you

Prayer

Lord, there are days when I don't feel it in my head or in my heart, but I make a commitment from this day forward to praise you! I ask that you forgive me for the times I have despised others for their extravagant displays of affection in worship. I will choose to act in faith and trust that as I worship you extravagantly you go before me and fight my battles. In Jesus name. Amen!

Selah
Pause • Wait • Meditate • Listen

"From now on, worshiping the Father will not be a matter of the right place, but with a right heart. For God is a Spirit, and he longs to have sincere worshipers who adore him in the realm of the Spirit and in truth." John 4:23-24 TPT

Decree

I decree that my praise is a weapon that destroys every demonic tactic, yoke, snare, and strategy against me and my loved ones.

I decree I am a worship warrior, and my worship is not hindered by my worries or emotions.

I decree my worship is dictated by God's worthiness to be praised.

I decree I offer up sacrificial praise because Jesus sacrificed his life for me.

I decree that I have the anointing of King David who was a man after God's own heart because of his willingness to be an undignified worshipper.

I decree I find myself singing hymns and spiritual songs all the time!

I decree Holy Spirit speaks to me through music constantly. I decree the Lord wakes me in the morning and sings a song to my spirit.

I decree that every demonic frequency sent to cause discord in my life is neutralized, NOW in the name of Jesus.

I decree that when I worship, God's glory fills the room and miracles break out spontaneously.

Jehovah Shammah Daddy is here

DAY 19

Arise and shine, dear one! I have watched over you all night long with my eyes of love, waiting for you to rise and turn your heart to me. Do you know that I look forward to your voice? In fact, I absolutely love the sound of your voice. Your sweet worship thrills my heart and draws me near. Your tender heartfelt prayers mean so much to me. I strongly desire for you to speak to me. When you pour out your heart at my feet, I am compelled to pour out answers to your prayers from the abundance of my glory. Like a fragrant perfume, your life is a pleasing aroma to me day and night. I am igniting in your heart a new passion for prayer and intercession. My Spirit will pray through you, and it will not be a burden, but a blessed time of intimacy between us. I want you to understand me the way I also understand you. Spend this time to come and see what I say. Write down what I speak to you. Ask for wisdom and revelation and I will give it to you liberally! Together we will manifest heavens solutions to the issues here on Earth that are burning in your heart to be reformed.

Love, Daddy God who loves to listen to you

Prayer

Lord, what a wonderful mystery it is to know that in all your power and sovereignty you choose to partner with the prayers of your people. Please help me to pray from the center of your will, rather than from my own self-centeredness. When I don't know what to pray, I ask you, Holy Spirit, to pray through me by giving me words and utterances directly from the Father's heart. In Jesus name. Amen!

Selah
Pause • Wait • Meditate • Listen

"Find your delight and true pleasure in Yahweh, and he will give you what you desire the most." Psalms 37:4 TPT

Decree

I decree I have a special grace to pray without ceasing. I decree my spirit is in constant communication with God, and he loves to respond to my prayers.

I decree my prayers are powerful, passionate, and effective.

I decree I do not pray self-centered prayers to manipulate God to get what I want; instead, I only pray to build relationship with God, and release what is his perfect will in every situation.

I decree I witness unusual and swift answers to prayer when my heart is in alignment with his heart.

I decree that prayer is as natural and easy as talking on the phone with my best friend.

I decree Jesus is a friend that is closer than a brother.

I decree when God gives me instructions in prayer, I am willing and faithful to follow through with what he says.

I decree I receive God's solutions to problems when I pray. I decree that I release forgiveness quickly when offended so that my prayers are not hindered.

I decree I am a happy intercessor who prays bold, outrageous prayers, full of faith!

Jehovah Shammah Daddy is here

DAY 20

I have called you to live and walk by faith. I want the portion of faith I have given you to grow and expand so that you can operate fully as a mature child of God. Do not just rely on your own faith, ask me for MORE! I desire to give you the gift of faith which is the revelation of the faith of Christ and the assurance of all the resources of heaven. This faith will keep you from sinking in a shaking and sifting world. You may wobble for a moment as you step out to act on your faith, but trust that I will meet you at the place of risk! Just as Peter walked on the waves as he focused on Jesus, you too will overcome the waves of the world as you step out in faith. The sea of circumstances that once threatened to drown you will become a wide-open place for you to run with me. Where there was a sea of trouble, there is now a sea of endless possibilities! The people around you will be amazed and be drawn to me because they will see how my Spirit in you has made you overcome all odds. Rejoice knowing that truly nothing is impossible with me! The boundaries are broken and there is no limit to how far you can go now as you walk by faith into my best plans for your future!

Love, Daddy God who believes in you

Prayer

Father, I believe! But please help my unbelief! Thank you for the measure of faith you have given me. Help me recognize when a spirit of fear is trying to rob me from taking a risk and keep me from seeing you work a miracle. By your Spirit working in me, I ask that you continue to reveal the vastness of your love for me since faith works by my understanding of your perfect love for me. I choose to expect you to make the impossible possible, in and through, my life for your glory. In Jesus name. Amen!

Selah

Pause • Wait • Meditate • Listen

"Yahweh looks down in love, looking over all of Adam's sons and daughters. He's looking to see if there is anyone who acts wisely, any who are searching for God and wanting to please him." Psalms 14:2 TPT

Decree

I decree that I will exercise my faith by taking action to see the kingdom of God released around me.
I decree even when I feel that my faith is small, it is still mighty enough in Christ to release atomic power to move mountains.
I decree that my faith works by experiencing God's faithful love for me, and by being a conduit of his love to those around me.
I decree I have the gift of faith and I steward it wisely.
I decree nothing shall be impossible for me because all things are possible with God, and he is with me.
I decree I operate in the faith OF GOD, not just faith IN GOD, which is the same faith that Jesus operated in when he walked in his earthly ministry.
I decree My Father is faithful to do what he said he will do.
I decree that Jesus loves me and because he loves me, I trust him.
I decree I prove my trust in God by my actions.
I decree all of God's promises in scripture are available to me because I believe what he says is true.
I decree God is not a man, therefore he will never lie to me. He is perfect truth, and never changes his mind toward me.

Jehovah Shammah Daddy is here

DAY 21

You can give me all your broken pieces, all your weakness, all your messy places. You are safe with me in your vulnerability. I see that the desire of your heart is to know me more and to please me. I also see your anxious thoughts of falling short. Receive my refreshing words of love shower down on you today. You are forgiven and made innocent in my sight. Receive this truth today: I delight in you. Your acceptance of the blood of Jesus was, and always will be, efficient for my acceptance of you. My love for you is perfect and does not change. I have loved you with an everlasting love and I chose you among the nations to be mine forever. My promise through the blood of my Son, Jesus, is to always do good to those who love me and keep my commands. You are drenched in my loving kindness. Like a parched rose is strengthened by a summer rain, so your heart is strengthened as you meditate on my love for you. I invite you into our secret place of intimacy within your heart for it has become Eden to me and I look upon you as if you have never sinned. The answer to every problem is my presence, my word, and my love. Come and receive the solutions you need from my abundance.

Love, Daddy God who is good to you

Prayer

Father, you make everything so simple. Thank you for reminding me that Christianity is not about what I do for you to earn your love, but rather it isthat I am already 100 percent loved by you. What a wonderful grace this is that I don't have to earn your affection or forgiveness because, you freely give it! Knowing this makes me want to live a life that I know pleases you. I come to you today with a clean conscience, accepting that the blood of Jesus is enough for you to fully receive me. In Jesus name. Amen!

Selah
Pause • Wait • Meditate • Listen

"For by grace you have been saved by faith. Nothing you did could ever earn this salvation, for it was the love gift from God that brought us to Christ!" Ephesians 2:8 TPT

Decree

I decree that the presence of God is everything I need for every problem I will ever face.

I decree that when I go to be with the Lord, I don't go only interested in what he can give me, but my primary focus is to give him myself in burning devotion.

I decree the walls around my heart are being demolished as the Holy Spirit crashes over me.

I decree I meditate on the simple gospel, which is, "God so loved me that he gave his Son to save me, so I could be united with them forever."

I decree I am 100 percent loved and accepted by God. I cannot earn his approval. I already have it because he loves me.

I decree God gives me "beauty for ashes."

I decree I know the difference between conviction and condemnation.

I decree conviction is a gift from God because it is my Father's nature in me, calling me into my righteous identity and away from sin.

I decree that I renounce shame and condemnation and command them to be cast far from me, in Jesus' name.

I decree the enemy will no longer lead me into condemnation because I am in Christ.

Jehovah Shammah Daddy is here

DAY 22

I have given you the keys to the Kingdom. "Whatever you bind on earth will be bound in heaven and whatever you loose on earth will be loosed in heaven." I have given you power and authority to create with your faith and decree. I am inviting you today to come out of agreement with the enemy's negative narrative and rise up to bind him and loose MY WORD and MY NAME to create a POSITIVE REPORT, not only in your sphere of life, but also in the earth. You are to be my witness to the truth of my kingdom and not to bow down to lies or roll over in fear of destruction. Have I not said that I give my angels charge over you? My kingdom reigns. I AM the GOOD NEWS. If it is NOT good, then it is NOT me. My heavenly Hosts are waiting with anticipation, and often frustration, to send out the report that my people agree with. What report do you want to "loose" across the nation today, beloved? I give you permission to release the headline you want attached to your history in heaven.
Love, Daddy God who empowers you

Prayer

Father, thank you for the great honor, authority, and responsibility to release your will on Earth with my prayers and decrees. I repent for using my mouth to release the report of the enemy. I renounce every evil or idol word I have spoken, and I render it null and void, in Jesus' name. I come into agreement with your word which says that "you make all things work together for the good of those who love you." I love you. Help me to trust in your goodness, even when I don't understand. In Jesus name. Amen!

Selah
Pause • Wait • Meditate • Listen

"I will give you the keys of heaven's kingdom realm to forbid on earth that which is forbidden in heaven, and to release on earth that which is released in heaven." Matthew 16:19 TPT

Decree

I decree my mouth is a blessing and not a curse. I use my words wisely to build up people and shred demonic platforms.

I decree that my heart is full of the knowledge of God's goodness. It is like a heavenly treasure trove. When I open my mouth, the abundance of my heart is released to the poor and crushed in spirit.

I decree angels are released on assignment when I release the word of the Lord.

I decree I was made to co-rule and co-reign seated with Christ in heavenly places.

I decree when I speak the natural and spiritual realms respond. I decree Christ has given me authority over all the powers of darkness and I use my voice to enforce Jesus' victory on the cross over the enemy.

I decree I will not be moved in reaction to fear but will live in response to my good Father God and his word over every situation I face.

I decree I am a king priest, and my words are powerful.

I decree the perfect will of God over every aspect of my life, family, and community today, in Jesus' name.

Jehovah Shammah Daddy is here

DAY 23

Would you take time to slow down and just breathe? I am in the breath; for your breath originated from me. In the beginning, I came down and I fashioned human beings from the earth. I loved the world so much I kissed the mud as I held it in my hands, and the love in my breath became a living expression in the form of the first man, Adam. The first thing Adam saw, when he opened his eyes, was my unveiled face hovering over his. The devastation of the Fall was truly the veil that sin created to separate you from my glory. This is why I sent my Son to restore what was lost through Adam's sin: face to face, mouth to mouth, breath to breath, heart to heart, communion with my children again. The finished work on the cross tore the veil from top to bottom in the temple as a sign that the heavens were open, and we could be reunited. You were created for union with me, and it all begins in returning to the place where my kiss first awakened your soul and you saw my love over you for the first time. It is time to slow down and just breathe, and return; be reunited with an unveiled face to behold my beauty.

Love, Daddy God who planned for you

Prayer

Lord, I could never forget the moment you rescued me, and I tasted of your love when I first believed. Help me to remember that my mission in life is to mirror you. To gaze upon your beauty and reflect the light of your presence just as Moses did when he met you face to face on the mountain. Thank you for tearing the veil so there is no longer any separation between us. In Jesus name. Amen!

Selah
Pause • Wait • Meditate • Listen

"We can all draw close to him with the veil removed from our faces. And with no veil we all become like mirrors who brightly reflect the glory of the Lord Jesus. We are being transfigured into his very image as we move from one brighter level of glory to another. And this glorious transfiguration comes from the Lord, who is the Spirit." 2 Corinthians 3:18 TPT

Decree

I decree I can boldly come before the throne of grace when I am in need.
I decree that I see God in every little thing that enters my experience.
I decree that all of life is a manifestation of God's love and desire to be with me.
I decree that as I surrender my mess to God, He takes it in his hands and makes it something beautiful.
I decree I renounce every lie that says that I am separated from God.
I decree I am separated from sin and one with Christ by his Spirit.
I decree Holy Spirit is constantly unveiling the beauty of Jesus to me.
I decree my life is an act of worship and everything I do, I do it for God's glory.
I decree when I pray, I am speaking face to face, mouth to mouth with my creator.
I decree my heart is open to God's truth.
I decree I am constantly being filled with the knowledge of God and his omnipresence in every moment of my life.

Jehovah Shammah Daddy is here

DAY 24

Come away with me and step into the higher place; ascend the stairway into the stars. My love for you is so immense. It is vaster than the earth and taller than the distance between Pluto and the sun. In fact, the universe is constantly expanding because it is a prophetic picture of my unending love for you. Right when you think you have discovered the end of my love, you discover an entirely new dimension of my heart for you. Against the cosmos you may feel small, like a grain of sand falling through the sands of time and space. But know that even amidst all the vastness of space I see you and know you and every detail of your life intimately and I my thoughts toward you are more numerous than the grains of sand or the stars in the sky. Your life is my delight and regardless of how small you feel, know that I have found great pleasure in putting the fullness of my Spirit in you.

Love, Daddy God who always thinks of you

Prayer

Father, your kindness, mercy and compassion never cease to amaze me. When I feel overlooked and underappreciated you are there watching over me and admiring all I do from a pure heart. Help me to surrender more and more to the explosive power of your Spirit that works within me so that I can grow into the giant of faith you created me to be. In Jesus name. Amen!

Selah
Pause • Wait • Meditate • Listen

"Then you will be empowered to discover what every holy one experiences, the great magnitude of the astonishing love of Christ in all its dimensions. How deeply intimate and far-reaching is his love! How enduring and inclusive it is! Endless love beyond measurement that transcends our understanding, this extravagant love pours into you until you are filled to overflowing with the fullness of God!" Ephesians 3:18-19

Decree

I decree that every spirit that would try to keep me small, must be removed from my life, now, in Jesus' name!
I decree my spiritual eyes and ears are open and alert to the spiritual world around me because I am naturally supernatural.
I decree I am growing and going from glory to glory by the power of God's spirit that works within me.
I decree my understanding and intimacy with God is ever expanding.
I decree I can go as deep as I desire into the mysteries of God's Kingdom.
I decree God's love for me and through me is limitless. I decree I am filled to overflowing with the fullness of God.
I decree when I seek the Lord with all my heart, I will find him, and he will show me great and mighty things that I have never seen before.
I decree that the eyes of my heart would be illuminated to reveal the hope of my calling in Christ Jesus.
I decree the Spirit within me is bigger than my body and it can enter the realms of heaven that are inaccessible to the flesh.

Jehovah Shammah Daddy is here

DAY 25

There you are, my darling, my friend! My heart is thrilled each time you come to meet with me. I am never indifferent towards you; quite the contrary, I am always intimately interested in every detail of your life. I wait eagerly for you to open the door of your heart to invite me into your day. As you receive my instruction, you are given my divine enablement to walk down the best path for your life. My words, both written and freshly spoken, become lamp posts that light your way and displace confusion, fear, and anxiety. Know this: you never have to fear the darkness when I, the Light of the world, am with you. As you walk in fellowship with the light, you are unable to remain in fellowship with darkness. Darkness cannot put up a fight with the light! It simply flees! So, stay in communication with me and my words to you will keep your heart on fire for me.
Love, Daddy God who gives you courage

Prayer

Father, you know my anxious thoughts and my overwhelming desire to please you because I love you so much. It is such a relief to know that when I don't know which path to take, your word releases light to show me the way! Thank you, Lord that I am found in you, and you will not leave me lost or alone on this journey called life. In Jesus name. Amen!

Selah
Pause • Wait • Meditate • Listen

"Then Jesus said, "I am light to the world, and those who embrace me will experience life-giving light, and they will never walk in darkness." John 8:12 TPT

Decree

I decree I have a spirit of revelation, wisdom, and knowledge to read and comprehend scripture.

I decree I am addicted to reading, hearing, and decreeing the word of God - both written and prophetically inspired.

I decree it is a passion of mine to know the word and meditate on it day and night.

I decree Holy Spirit partners with me as I read and interpret scripture, so I am always discovering hidden treasures, deep secrets and spiritual mysteries that make Bible reading fun and exciting!

I decree that I have ears to hear, eyes to see and the mind of Christ to discern what the Lord is saying.

I decree that I do not despise prophecy, but I earnestly pursue operating in that spiritual gift.

I decree I will fulfill what God has written about me in my destiny scroll.

I decree I am a hero in heaven because I trust God.

I decree because I honor God's prophets, I receive an impartation of their gift and anointing according to God's will to reward me.

Jehovah Shammah Daddy is here

DAY 26

Do you know that I know you? That I know who you really are deep down inside at the core of your being? You should not cringe or feel insecure hearing this. I know the lie of the enemy has caused you to feel that if you were really, truly known by others, then you would be rejected by them. Oh child, this is a great deception! Since your salvation, at the core of who you are, there is Christ. He is one with you, the hope of glory. You are not rotten to the core; you are GOOD, and you ooze my glory everywhere you go! Difficulties are simply opportunities for me to train you in righteousness. When you see something in you that doesn't look like me, I will remind you who I made you to be in Christ. As you remember who you really are all the lies and false identities will be replaced with the fullness of my character and nature. You were made for love and as you abide in me, I will abide in you, and you will naturally produce more of my character and nature.
Love, Daddy God who likes you

Prayer

Lord thank you for knowing me and pruning every area of my life that doesn't line up with who I am in Christ. Release an increase of grace to be securely abiding in your life. That my roots would be anchored in your love and others may taste and see you through our union. In Jesus name. Amen!

Selah
Pause • Wait • Meditate • Listen

"God saw everything that He had made, and behold, it was very good, and He validated it completely. And there was evening and there was morning, a sixth day." Genesis 1:31 AMP

Decree

I decree I am fully known and fully loved by my wonderful heavenly Father.

I decree I am good because God is in me, and he is good. I decree I am validated by my Father God.

I decree it's not I who lives, but Christ lives his life through me.

I decree that I produce the fruit of the Spirit, which is love, joy, peace, patience, goodness, gentleness, and self-control.

I decree virtues are multiplying in me daily as I focus on relationship with Jesus.

I decree that God has permission to cut out of my life anything that is hindering the life of his Spirit coming to full bloom through me, in Jesus' name.

I decree I am his carefully cultivated garden. I decree tares, canker worms, and bitter roots have no place in me as I continue to give more and more space to the Lord in my heart, mind, and life.

I decree God is restoring the years that the locusts have eaten as if they were never there.

Jehovah Shammah Daddy is here

DAY 27

Do you know that I am the God who dances and sings over you with joy? It isso important for you to know that I am not angry with you. I have judged your sin on the cross and I am no longer at war with man. I am only at war with anything that gets in between your ability to have relationship with me. Know also, my child, that I do not war in the same way that flesh and bone make war. I destroyed all the works of darkness by revealing the light of my goodness and glory through my self-sacrificing love poured out on Calvary. In my house you do not have to walk on eggshells, worrying about upsetting me. My wrath against sin was poured out on the cross. I am not mad at you. Now, let me teach you how to dance and play with me. Instead of looking down at your feet in an effort to plan your next move, look into my eyes and come into the rhythm of my song over you. You are free to smile back at me and laugh! In my presence is fullness of joy and pleasures at my right hand forever because you are seated with Christ at my right hand! That's right! You with me, in my Son, Jesus, are my eternal pleasure! It is my delight to lead you into this joy because I love you.

Love, Daddy God who delights in you

Prayer

Father, I want more than anything to discover this unspeakable joy of knowing you. I am so delighted to lean in deeper to your loving support. Please teach me how to play with you so I can enjoy glorious fellowship with you. I can do nothing apart from you. Thank you, Father, for restoring me to childlike innocence again! In Jesus name. Amen!

Selah
Pause • Wait • Meditate • Listen

"Lord, you are my secret hiding place, protecting me from these troubles, surrounding me with songs of gladness! Your joyous shouts of rescue release my breakthrough. Pause in his presence"
Psalms 32:7 TPT

Decree

I decree I am anointed with the oil of joy for mourning. I decree God greatly rejoices over me.
I decree that I am not a burden, but a blessing. I decree my Father God sits in the heavens and laughs, and I laugh with him!
I decree seriousness is not a fruit of the spirit; joy is!
I decree I am known for my joy because I was the joy set before Christ on the other side of the cross.
I decree the Lord delights to carry me when I cannot carry the load myself.
I decree I break agreement with every false burden, unrealistic expectation and hindering demon, that would yoke me to heaviness and depression, in Jesus' name.
I decree the Lord delights in me, and I am free to delight myself in him. **I decree** as I delight myself in the Lord, he gives me the desires of my heart.

Jehovah Shammah Daddy is here

DAY 28

I have seen you in the battle, my Beloved. The enemy has launched attacks against you to attempt to thwart your destiny, in hopes that you will retreat and surrender the territory you have taken from him. When I called you into my kingdom, I gave you a promise that you would overtake the enemy and recover ALL that he stole from you. I hate robbery and injustice. The enemy comes to kill, steal, and destroy, but I came to give you an abundant life! When you enter spiritual warfare, it is not because I am punishing you. It is because the enemy is afraid of the destiny, I have placed on the inside of you. Do not throw in the towel or surrender to bitterness because of the battle. That is a demonic tactic sent to manipulate my people into aborting their destiny. Rise up, oh warrior, shake off your shame and stand your ground, for I am the Lord who declares only victory for you!

Love, Daddy God who fights for you

Prayer

Father, please forgive me for anytime I have believed the lie that when I am going through a battle, it is because you are punishing me. I reject and renounce that lie, and I receive your victory and abundant life now. I say that the suffering of Jesus was the punishment for my sin. The cross was and always will be enough for me. Anoint me with strength to overcome the battle and become more like you in the process. In Jesus name. Amen!

Selah
Pause • Wait • Meditate • Listen

"Your hand-to-hand combat is not with human beings, but with the highest principalities and authorities operating in rebellion under the heavenly realms. For they are a powerful class of demon-gods and evil spirits that hold this dark world in bondage." Ephesians 6:12 TPT

Decree

I decree that I am advancing in my divine destiny in Christ.
I decree that I will pursue the high call of Christ and take back everything the enemy stole from me.
I decree that every diabolical assignment sent to cause premature death to me, my property, my prosperity, my family, my ministry, and my destiny, is destroyed, now, in the name of Jesus.
I decree that life abundant is my portion in Christ and I release resurrection life over myself, my property, my prosperity, my family, my ministry, and my destiny, in Jesus' name.
I decree challenges are opportunities for God to showcase His glory through my life.
I decree I renounce every spirit of suspicion, in Jesus' name.
I decree God has permission to sanctify my gift of discernment and to give me wisdom and conviction to not war with people, but to war according to the spirit.
I decree I put on the full armor of God to stand against the enemy.
I decree I am not a quitter; I am more than a conqueror through Christ

Jehovah Shammah Daddy is here

DAY 29

I will never allow you to enter a battle that I have not equipped you to win with me by your side. I have given you authority to call on angelic reinforcement to aid you in the battle, and over all the powers of darkness that would try to come against you. Pick up your authority! Use what I have given you and release yourself from the false burden that you are in this alone. I am opening your eyes to see that there are more for you than are against you! So, do not be discouraged or dismayed. Have I not told you to be bold and very courageous because I the Lord go with you to occupy your inheritance? You are enlisted in my army and have been preordained to be more than a conqueror through Christ who lives in you. Release your need to defend yourself and I will be your defense. Submit again to being conquered by my love in a deeper way than you have ever experienced before. As you remember my love, all your fears will melt away. Lean in, ask for more understanding of my love, for my love is the fire that will fuel you in the days ahead.
Love, Daddy God who cheers you on

Prayer

Lord, I repent for surrendering my authority out of a lack of confidence in who I am in you and a lack of understanding of all you have given me in Christ. I ask for forgiveness and ask for you to teach me more about what it means to have dominion. Now I pick up my authority to overcome all the powers of darkness for your glory Father! In Jesus name. Amen!

Selah
Pause • Wait • Meditate • Listen

"Jesus said "You must continually bring healing to lepers and to those who are sick and make it your habit to break off the demonic presence from people, and raise the dead back to life. Freely you have received the power of the kingdom, so freely release it to others." Matthew 10:8 TPT

Decree

I decree I have been given authority over all the powers of darkness.
I decree I repent for wherever I have sat down, or surrendered my authority to the enemy, and I command it be returned to me now with interest, in Jesus' name.
I decree that angels are being sent now to assist me when needed, according to the word of the Lord.
I decree God turns what the enemy meant to harm me into outrageous opportunities to bless me!
I decree that I always come out better after every battle! I decree I am blessed and highly favored by God.
I decree casting out demons is easy and fun. They have to shut up and get out when I used the name of Jesus and the authority, he gave me.
I decree when I pray for people, they receive breakthrough.
I decree I am a walking God encounter! When people encounter me, they encounter God with me!
I decree I will not be blinded by the activity of the enemy.
I decree I live in response to the Father, not in reaction to the enemy.

Jehovah Shammah Daddy is here

DAY 30

Know this, I take what the enemy meant for evil and make his plans backfire in his face, causing it to work for your good! As you lean into my love, my ways, my hope, and my promises over your life you will be divinely empowered to weather every storm and siege from the enemy. Just as a muscle being exercised increases in strength and endurance, the exercising of your faith in this season has increased your spiritual strength and produced the endurance needed to withstand the weight of glory I desire to place on you in the season to come. I have made your battle ground to become your training ground to teach you how to take ground for my kingdom. It is for this reason you can greatly rejoice, even in the battle, knowing that I am working what was sent to destroy you, to be a blessing to you in the end. No weapon formed against you will be successful to accomplish what it was sent to do. Instead, it will perfect your character and solidify the high call of Christ that I placed on the inside you.
Love, Daddy God who cheers you on

Prayer

Father, difficulties in life are never fun, but I know they are often required for me to exercise my faith in you. Help me to see problems as a pathway to joy, knowing that when I pass the test before me, I will receive a crown of victory and the untold blessings that you have promised to all your faithful lovers. In Jesus name. Amen!

Selah
Pause • Wait • Meditate • Listen

"And to the one who conquers I will give the privilege of sitting with me on my throne, just as I conquered and sat down with my Father on his throne." Revelation 3:21 TPT

Decree

I decree that I discover the opportunity for indescribable joy in the face of difficulty because I know God is training my inner man to carry more of his glory.
I decree that I know the difference between testing and temptation, and I ask God for greater wisdom to discern between the two.
I decree I am not controlled by the lusts of my flesh, but my body is in submission to my spirit.
I decree God does not tempt me with sinful desires.
I decree that all the plans of the enemy against my life and my loved ones are backfiring in his face.
I decree my battle ground will be a training ground for me to take ground for the Kingdom.
I decree the Lord will even make my enemies rise up and call me blessed.
I decree I will not allow my anger to lead me to sin, nor will I give the enemy a foothold in my life when I am angry.
I decree Jesus is the master of my emotions.
I decree no weapon formed against me will be successful and every tongue that rises against me I will condemn, as this is my inheritance in the Lord.

Jehovah Shammah Daddy is here

DAY 31

Is your heart hurting from the wounds inflicted by the "accusation" arrows of friendly fire? Have you taken hits because of slander and gossip? Have you been misunderstood and rejected for my name's sake? Beloved, you are beyond blessed to share in the sufferings of Christ who endured all this, and more, for the joy of having you as our own on the other side of the Cross. In order to experience the power of the resurrection there must be a death to self. Do you feel as if part of you has died in this last season? Oh! what joy awaits you, for I am releasing resurrection power into every lifeless area of your heart! I came to heal the broken hearted and bind their wounds. I will not leave you how I found you. Just as fire refines and purifies gold, the fires of adversity will always cause you to come out better on the other side than how you went in. Purification is a prelude to promotion. You cannot go to the next place weak and wounded. Please bring me your battle wounds; for it is in my wounds that you are healed.

Love, Daddy God who understands you

Prayer

Lord, when I think about you hanging naked and ashamed on the Cross just for me, I am overwhelmed by gratitude. My healing is in your wounds and on the third day your resurrection became my resurrection too. What an honor it is to share in a small way the suffering you endured for me. It is in this place that I find a greater understanding of who you are and just how much you love me. In Jesus name. Amen!

Selah
Pause • Wait • Meditate • Listen

"But He was wounded for our transgressions, He was crushed for our wickedness [our sin, our injustice, our wrongdoing]; The punishment [required] for our well-being fell on Him, And by His stripes (wounds) we are healed." Isaiah 53:5 AMP

Decree

I decree that I release forgiveness to those who have wounded me. Father, forgive them, because they don't know what they are doing.

I decree that resurrection life is being released over every dead area of my heart and life, now. In Jesus name!

I decree that love holds no record of wrongs. Therefore, I refuse to hold any record that enforces bitterness or justification for my own sin toward another person.

I decree I am beloved, and I belong in God's family. I decree that my heart is soft toward the Lord, toward myself, and toward others.

I decree I am fully known and fully loved by God.

I decree by the stripes of Jesus I am healed. I decree that as I submit myself to the Refiner's fire, the purification of my character will produce endurance and promotion in due time.

I decree I don't get bitter; I get better! I decree that every spirit of backlash and retaliation is broke off me now and must go to the pit! In Jesus name!

I decree I am humble and quick to receive correction. As a result, I am growing in increasing wisdom.

Jehovah Shammah Daddy is here

DAY 32

Trust and believe I have never been defeated. I am the King of Victory, not the King of Victims. I became a victim in your place on the Cross so that I could give you a new identity as a victor through me. I want this truth to so deeply sink into your heart that it becomes a part of you: There is no trial, test, or battle that I will ever allow you to enter without your predetermined victory and total healing already being established. This complete salvation, healing and deliverance belongs to you, but you must be willing to take hold of it and enforce my victory won on the Cross by applying my blood and my word to your life for you to receive all its benefits. I AM the Lord your God who fights your battles for you as you simply stay connected to me in quiet confidence. You will watch as we subdue every enemy under our feet for, I AM the God who stands up for my people! Together we will collect the spoils of war and share the strategies of your own private victories with those who are struggling in their own battles.

Love, Daddy God who stands up for you

Prayer

Father, thank you for securing my total healing, deliverance, and salvation! You are a strong place I can run into and find safety for my soul. Under your wings I find shelter and courage to stand against the enemy and enforce the victory you already won for me! In Jesus name. Amen!

Selah
Pause • Wait • Meditate • Listen

"As for us, we have all of these great witnesses who encircle us like clouds. So, we must let go of every wound that has pierced us and the sin we so easily fall into. Then we will be able to run life's marathon race with passion and determination, for the path has been already marked out before us." Hebrews 12:1 TPT

Decree

I decree that I receive all the benefits of the precious blood of Jesus over my life.

I decree the DNA of my Father God is overwriting the corrupted DNA of my human ancestors.

I decree the blood of Jesus pleads a better word than the blood of my ancestors.

I decree that I renounce every spirit passed down to me through generational sin and iniquity, and command it to be broken off me and my children forever onward.

I decree the blood of Jesus has nullified every generational curse in my bloodline.

I decree I will pick up the torch my forefathers dropped and carry on my family's God ordained destiny and assignment to completion.

I decree I receive my spiritual inheritance through God to accomplish the mandate on my life.

I decree the blood of Jesus has opened long awaited generational promises and blessings to me and my offspring.

I decree I read and apply the word of God to my life, because the Word of Life has power to continually deliver me.

Jehovah Shammah Daddy is here

DAY 33

My deep desire, darling, is for you to be securely rooted and anchored in my unmovable steadfast love for you. The very bedrock of your faith must be my love, for all other foundations are like shifting sands. The gospel is not complicated. How I want my church to return to the simple gospel! And that simple gospel is that God loved mankind and desired to be one with them! Relationship with you is my aim. To be entangled with you in intimate fellowship is what my heart longs for. A tree is only as secure as its root system. When you are deeply planted in my love the storms of life will not be able to uproot you. Instead, you will be safe and secure like a mighty oak of Lebanon, a planting of my splendor to show all the world that no matter the consequences, in my love you can be safe, strong, and weather any storm. Today dig deep into me and stretch your arms wide to receive more of my embrace. Lift your face up to my shining face and be confident that when the systems of the world sink like sand into the sea, you, my love, are like a tree planted by the river of life securely anchored on a firm foundation, which is me.
Love, Daddy God who keeps you safe

Prayer

God, thank you for picking me up and placing my feet on solid ground. I want so much to be securely rooted in your love. I ask that you release more grace to me to grow deeper in my union with you. I open myself up to be nurtured by your love so that I can be a mature believer in Christ for your glory. In Jesus name. Amen!

Selah
Pause • Wait • Meditate • Listen

"Since we are now joined to Christ, we have been given the treasures of redemption by his blood—the total cancellation of our sins—all because of the cascading riches of his grace." Ephesians 1:7 TPT

Decree

I decree that I come out of agreement with any foundation that is not Christ and his love for me.
I decree that my life is built on the love of God and Christ's righteousness.
I decree I am safe and secure because Jesus loves me.
I decree when the storms of life come my faith becomes stronger because I press deeper into God's presence.
I decree that I find great strength as I meditate on God's word day and night.
I decree I delight to bathe myself in scripture reading. As I read, I am refreshed and restored.
I decree I am honest and reliable. My "yes" is my yes, and my "no" is my no.
I decree I am delivered from every spirit of domination, witchcraft, manipulation, control, and fear of man, now. In Jesus name!
I decree every mind binding and mind blinding spirit, along with every spirit of confusion and brain fog, must go and be replaced with the mind of Christ, now. In Jesus name!
I decree I am not a people pleaser; I am a God pleaser!

Jehovah Shammah Daddy is here

DAY 34

I have commissioned you to produce lasting fruit. It is only in union with me that you can truly thrive and produce the fruit of my Spirit, which is love in all its various expressions. You will recognize where you are rooted depending on the fruit you produce. Examine your fruit today, dear one. Are you exuding the fruit of my spirit which is love, joy, peace, patience, goodness, gentleness, kindness, and self-control? Or are you harboring the fruit of the flesh, which is unforgiveness, bitterness, jealousy, strife, angry outbursts, self-centeredness, criticism, gossip, and anxiety? Flesh fruits are not found when you are securely anchored in my root of love, because the flesh is at enmity with the spirit. A mindset focused on the flesh is separated from me, and apart from me you can do nothing. As you grow more aware of your connection to me you can produce my fruit. The axe has been laid at the root of the tree of the knowledge of good and evil and you are invited to come feast on me. I am the tree of life budding within you whose leaves are for the healing of the nations. Feast on my fruit of love and take me in; take on my nature.

Love, Daddy God your new family tree

Prayer

Father, I know that apart from you I can do nothing. I know that everything I need for life and godliness come from you. Today I release the axe of your word to chop down the tree of the knowledge of good and evil that produces cycles of corruption in my life. I ask for your fire to consume me until I am made one with you. In Jesus name. Amen!

Selah
Pause • Wait • Meditate • Listen

"Gaze upon him, join your life with his, and joy will come. Your faces will glisten with glory. You'll never wear that shame-face again." Psalms 34:5 TPT

Decree

I decree that I am growing in constant awareness of your life dwelling on the inside of me.
I decree that my mind is fixed on Jesus.
I decree Jesus is my obsession and I simply cannot get enough of him!
I decree I was created for devotion to Christ alone.
I decree God's perfect order be released over my life. In Jesus name. I decree Jesus comes first and has preeminence in all things relating to my heart and life.
I decree I have abundant grace to have and experience as much of God and his Kingdom as I desire.
I decree I abide in Christ, and I produce fruit that remains.
I decree when people see my life, they get a taste of just how good my Daddy God is!
I decree my life is full of love, joy, peace, patience, gentleness, kindness, goodness and self-control.
I decree I produce so much of the fruit of the Spirit that I am constantly finding hungry souls to give my fruit to so they can taste and see how good my God is!

Jehovah Shammah Daddy is here

DAY 35

I have come as you have asked to draw you to my heart and bring you into my fullness. The garden within you is so beautiful and bright with blossoming flowers! Now the season for singing and pruning the vines has arrived. I tenderly lift each branch connected to me that doesn't bear fruit and I prune every fruit bearing branch to produce more. I know the pruning can seem painful, my love, but it is necessary for you to grow into greater maturity. As every good and loving father corrects the children he loves, so do I. But I do not traffic in fear, shame, and condemnation. No, I simply remind you that you are my child and as my child you reflect me. If you don't see it in me, then it should not be in you. Do you see now that I only remove from you what is hindering your growth into the person, I created you to be? The early signs of my purposes and plans are ready to burst forth from within you. Soon the budding vines of your new life in Christ will be blooming everywhere. The fragrance of their flowers whisper, "There is change in the air," as you are being transformed by love.

Love, Daddy God who corrects and redirects you

Prayer

You are such a good Father, God. You are never angry or harsh toward me. I don't need to fear your correction or discipline in my life because your perfect love for me drives out all fear of punishment. I will praise you in each season of pruning, knowing that you are getting rid of everything in me that doesn't look like you and making space for more of you and your divine purposes for my life to come into fruition. In Jesus name. Amen!

Selah
Pause • Wait • Meditate • Listen

"For it was always in his perfect plan to adopt us as his delightful children, through our union with Jesus, the Anointed One, so that his tremendous love that cascades over us would glorify his grace —for the same love he has for the Beloved, Jesus, he has for us. And this unfolding plan brings him great pleasure!" Ephesians 1:5-6 TPT

Decree

I decree I know God as my perfect and loving Father.

I decree that there is no fear in love. God's perfect love, for me, casts out of my soul any fear of God's punishment when I stumble.

I decree God does not punish me. He punished my sin on the cross and now he says I am innocent.

I decree that I have a reverence and deep respect for my Father God that is the foundation of all wisdom.

I decree that I forgive my earthly father for anyway that he failed to reveal the true heart of Father God to me. I bless him and release him, now. In Jesus name!

I decree that I sever from me now every relationship, mindset, connection, agreement, and false belief system that is hindering me from going to my next place.

I decree when I turn away from sin and turn to my Father God, he is quick, not only to forgive me, but to forget about my sin.

I decree I am not a victim! I reject a victim mentality and I receive a victor's reality, now. In Jesus name!

I decree when the Father looks at me through the blood of Jesus, it's as if I never sinned.

I decree the same love God has for Jesus he also has for me.

Jehovah Shammah Daddy is here

DAY 36

When I look at you, I see how you have taken my fruit and tasted my word. Your life has become clean and pure, like a lamb washed and newly shorn. You now show grace and balance with truth on display. I am so pleased with you. Like a royal diadem in my hand, certainly of all creation, you are my crowning achievement. You are my beautifully cultivated garden, my private paradise, where I can dwell among the lilies. Let me teach you how to keep the garden of your heart free from weeds and thorns. You must guard your heart above all things because from it flow the issues of life. When you guard your heart, you are not closing it off from those around you. It is important for you to keep your heart open to love, even the unlovable, because love is what changes the world. After all, my love is what changed you, remember? When you guard your heart, you are quick to do away with all lies and deception, offenses, bitterness, jealousy, and unforgiveness. When weedy seeds try to take root, be quick to take them captive and pluck them out. Do this as often as they come, and I will give you beautiful truths to plant in their place so that you can continue to blossom and thrive.

Love, Daddy God who is vulnerable with you

Prayer

Father, thank you for loving me enough to show me the areas of my heart that need healed and set free. Please show me any place where lies and trauma have given birth to bitter roots. I want to be quick to weed them out and replace them with your beautiful truths. In Jesus name. Amen!

Selah
Pause • Wait • Meditate • Listen

"You live fully in me and now I live fully in them so that they will experience perfect unity, and the world will be convinced that you have sent me, for they will see that you love each one of them with the same passionate love that you have for me." John 17:23 TPT

Decree

I decree that I make allowances for the faults of others and forgive quickly, because God forgave me.
I decree that I am not easily offended.
I decree that as I grow in intimacy with God, I am learning how to grow in intimacy with the people close to me.
I decree that my love for others is based on how God loves me and not based on how they love me.
I decree I am my Daddy God's crowning achievement.
I decree I am aware of God's pleasure over me.
I decree the Holy Spirit can help me understand God's incredible love for me and do exceedingly and abundantly more through me than I can ask or imagine in my ability to love others.
I decree that I welcome opportunities to grow in humility.
I decree jealousy and competition have no place in me.
I decree I am one with my brothers and sisters in Christ. When one of us advances, we all advance; when they win, I win.
I decree when feelings of inferiority try to rise in me, I respond in the opposite Spirit, enthusiastically cheering on the people I see God promoting.

Jehovah Shammah Daddy is here

DAY 37

I want you to take time in my arms and stay here with me in this moment. Practice the art of binding your wandering heart and mind to me. I see your mind race off to the future, or after glimmering distractions, when you come to speak with me. I am not frustrated when this happens in our time together. I am slow to anger, incredibly patient and easy to please. You forget so easy I am well pleased with you, my child, and you are not in trouble with me. Just as a father pursues a fleeing toddler, no matter where you run, my goodness and mercy are always chasing you down. When your mind wanders off don't beat yourself up, because I certainly do not. Learn from me and my ways. Be patient and gentle to yourself as I am patient and gentle with you. When your mind wanders go and fetch it and I will go with you to bring it back to where we left off in our conversation. Just because you lost focus of me does not mean I could ever lose sight of you. I am with you in the wandering and my Spirit is constantly pulling you back to be aware of my desire to communicate with you.
Love, Daddy God who communicates with you

Prayer

Father it's so true that my heart so desires to have unbroken fellowship with you and when I discover that I have been distracted during prayer I become frustrated with myself. Thank you for understanding me in my humanity. Your love and patience for me, right where I am, frees me to have patience with myself. Help me to reject performance-based Christianity, and to grow in the freedom of this beautiful relationship I have with you. In Jesus name. Amen!

Selah
Pause • Wait • Meditate • Listen

"My dearest one, let me tell you how I see you— you are so thrilling to me. To gaze upon you is like looking at one of Pharaoh's finest horses — a strong, regal steed pulling his royal chariot." Song of Songs 1:9 TPT

Decree

I decree even when my mother and father fail to love me, my Father God is quick to pick me up in his arms.

I decree goodness, mercy, and unprecedented blessings chase me down every day of my life.

I decree I am free to be at rest in God's love.

I decree God's love for me is not dependent on how much I produce or perform for him.

I decree I am growing in my ability to be still in God's presence.

I decree when I wait on the Lord, he renews my strength and lifts me up to soar above my circumstances.

I decree my heart is intertwined with God's heart and I am moved by the impulses of his Spirit.

I decree Holy Spirit prompts me into conversation and I am quick to respond to what he says.

I decree I am patient, gentle and kind to myself and to others because that is how my Father God is toward me.

I decree whether I am taking a nap or preaching the gospel in front of millions, God's love, and approval of me are the same.

I decree no more striving in my life from this day forward

Jehovah Shammah Daddy is here

DAY 38

Good morning, my mighty one! I know you might not feel mighty in this moment, but your feelings are not always factual. In fact, they can often be fickle, and they are always fleeting. This is why you must make choices in response to my word that never changes, rather than in reaction to your emotions that are always changing. So yes, I say that you are mighty in me and by my Spirit that lives inside of you. I have put creative power in your mouth to speak my word, and shift not just your emotions, but your reality. So, when you feel weak you can say, "I am strong." And when you are anxious, you can say, "I do not have a spirit of fear, but of love, power, and a sound mind." And when you are sick and broken, you can say, "By his stripes I am healed." When you feel rejected, you can say, "I am chosen by God." When you feel unloved you can say, "I am the beloved of the Lord." In light of this truth, use your voice to prophesy over yourself and those I have placed in your life. When what you see doesn't line up with what I say, then use the power I have delegated to you through a decree, and it will be established according to my will.
Love, Daddy God who blesses you

Prayer

Father your word is wonderful and powerful. One word spoken from your mouth can change my life. Your promises over me surpass my human emotions and mental reasoning. Continue to teach me how to use my mouth to speak your word and will into every situation with faith regardless of how I "feel." In Jesus name. Amen!

Selah
Pause • Wait • Meditate • Listen

"For who has ever intimately known the mind of the Lord Yahweh well enough to become his counselor? Christ has, and we possess Christ's perceptions." 1 Corinthians 2:16 TPT

Decree

I decree every tormenting spirit must shut up and be removed from my life, now. In Jesus name!

I decree my mind, will, and emotions must come into submission to the Spirit of God and the word of God, now. In Jesus name!

I decree that I consistently take every ungodly thought captive and I force it to obey Christ.

I decree I have the mind of Christ.

I decree I think God thoughts.

I decree I don't just have good ideas; I have God ideas.

I decree I can perceive God's imaginations.

I decree I say what I see and hear God is saying, even in difficult situations.

I decree I prosper in health even as my souls prospers. I decree I am excellent of soul.

I decree God's words are more powerful than my emotions.

Jehovah Shammah Daddy is here

DAY 39

You are so brave as you constantly yield yourself more and more to me. You have become a true warrior of love, my beautiful bride, who is dressed and ready for battle. "The weapons of your warfare are not carnal, but mighty to pull down strongholds." My love is your bow, and the gifts of the Spirit are your arrows to pierce even the hardest of hearts and take out the enemy operating within those you contact. My Spirit within you always releases the exact ammunition that you need when you need it. I have anointed you with the same Spirit of power that I anointed Jesus with who went about doing good, healing all who were oppressed by the devil and destroying all the works of darkness. You were prepared in the wilderness while you worshipped me. I have trained you for war and strengthened your arm to bend the bow, and now I am releasing you like a weapon into the world to be my witness. The gospel is not a matter of mere words, but of power! So today receive my power by faith to destroy hell. Do not be afraid for I will be with you and my Spirit will work with you to prove that I am who you say I am.
Love, Daddy God who shows up for you

Prayer

Father, thank you for sending us the promise and the presence of the Holy Spirit who is the third person of the Trinity! Holy Spirit forgive me if I have grieved or ignored you. I invite you to come and fill me with the nature of Christ. I ask that you please come upon me with fire and power so I can be your witness. I want to know you and to introduce others to you whenever I testify about Jesus. Teach me to work with you and honor your precious presence each moment of my life. In Jesus name. Amen!

Selah
Pause • Wait • Meditate • Listen

"But I promise you this—the Holy Spirit will come upon you, and you will be seized with power. You will be my messengers to Jerusalem, throughout Judea, the distant provinces —even to the remotest places on earth!" Acts 1:8 TPT

Decree

I decree that I am full of power and might by the Holy Spirit.
I decree I am growing increasingly aware of Holy Spirit with me.
I decree that I earnestly desire the Holy Spirit. he is not just a power; he is the third person of the Godhead who desires relationship with me.
I decree that I am sensitive to Holy Spirit's direction and leading. I decree Holy Spirit loves me and leads me into all truth.
I decree I am anointed and appointed to destroy the works of darkness by releasing the power of God's love and light.
I decree I believe in Jesus; therefore, signs and wonders follow me.
I decree I can trust Holy Spirit to show up and confirm the gospel for me when I take a risk in faith to pray for someone or tell someone about Jesus.
I decree I am anointed and appointed for such a time as this! I decree I am a powerful witness to how Jesus is.
I decree when I witness, people are supernaturally compelled to want to know how they can be saved too.
I decree Lord send me out to bring in your harvest of souls!

Jehovah Shammah Daddy is here

DAY 40

You are never separated from the wonders of my love for you. Don't get caught in the trap of wondering about what tomorrow will bring, for I am already there preparing the way for you. Don't entertain worldly worries and wondering about the care of your body, your family, or your future. In me is the fullness of everything you need. Enter my presence, jump into my arms, and ask me whatever it is that you need, and it will be done for you. You do not need to beg. All that is required of you is to trust and believe that you will receive what you ask for. Faith is the substance that is required to manifest your miracle in the natural. So, when your thoughts begin to wonder, and worry tries to overtake you, come back to the center of my heart. Trust that I am already in your tomorrow preparing all that you need right on time — because I love you. If you are to wonder at all, then look with wonder at the depth of my marvelous love that I have lavished on you! I have called you and made you my very own beloved child! I am a Father who takes care of my children. As you count all the ways I have cared for you, you will see you can continue to count on me to take care of you.

Love, Daddy God who takes care of you

Prayer

Father, release me from the cares of this life! Help me to see where I am depending on myself and my own means rather than trusting you to take care of me. I invite you to please come and remind me of all the times you have provided for me in the past. I trust that the same God who came through for me in the past will do it for me again and again whenever I am in need because you are good, and I know that you love me! In Jesus name. Amen!

Selah
Pause • Wait • Meditate • Listen

"Even the strong and the wealthy grow weak and hungry, but those who passionately pursue the Lord will never lack any good thing." Psalms 34:10 TPT

Decree

I decree that the spirit of poverty and lack is broken off me, now. In Jesus name!

I decree God's plans for me are good, for hope, and a future, and to prosper me in my final outcome.

I decree God gives me witty ideas, inventions, business ideas, and wisdom to gain wealth.

I decree I am blessed to be a blessing.

I decree when I am moved by God to give, I do it with a cheerful heart knowing that I can't out give God's ability to pay me back with interest.

I decree I am generous because my Father God is extravagantly generous. My generosity exhibits God's grace in such a way it makes people who experience it want to know who my God is.

I decree God alone is my provider and he will always provide exactly what I need right on time.

I decree repentance for anyway I have been a poor steward over the provision God has given me. I ask for God's forgiveness and command any curses withholding my blessing to be removed, now. In Jesus name!

ABOUT THE AUTHOR

Christa Elisha

Christa Elisha is a vibrant revivalist that burns with passionate devotion to Jesus. She is a rising prophetic voice to the nation, a social media influencer, artist, Elijah List author and the founder of Arise Kingdom Ministries, the Revival Rooms, and Lit Revolution. She has been featured in Charisma Magazine and is a frequent guest on Elijah Streams. Christa carries a strong anointing to invite others into the ecstatic bliss of knowing Christ for who he truly is: The only one who satisfies every need for every soul. It is out of this intimacy that she has been commissioned by God to baptize a generation in Holy Fire so that the bride of Christ arises in purity and power to shake the gates, destroy hell, and radiate the splendor of the risen King, bringing glory to the Father. She and her husband David are both anointed entrepreneurs and are leaders in their community. They have worked alongside of each other to advance the gospel, care for the poor and the unborn, equip the saints and to build unity among the churches. Together they are devoted to God, each other and their two beautiful children, Samariah and Arie. Currently they reside in Cincinnati Ohio but are frequently traveling while Christa preaches at revival crusades and other events around the nation. Christa walks in signs and wonders and prays that revival fire is sparked in each person she touches as her heart cries "On earth as it is in heaven!" To learn more about her ministry, check out her online store or find out where Christa is preaching next visit www.ChristaElisha.com To book her for an event email booking@christaelisha.co

Copyright Christa Elisha. Any Unauthorized reproduction or distribution of this material is strictly prohibited and punishable by law.